The  Home Makeover

The eBay™ Home Makeover

buying confidently,
redecorating with style—
the complete guide to
transforming your home online

Alyssa Ettinger

Principal Photography by Jennifer Lévy

WATSON-GUPTILL PUBLICATIONS / NEW YORK

Dedication

For my Dad—because I know watching me turn trash
into treasure, *as my job,* would have amused you.

Senior Acquisitions Editor: Victoria Craven
Project Editor: Anne McNamara
Developmental Editor: Chris Kincade
Associate Editor: Gayle Brosnan
Contributing Editors: Martha Moran, Melissa Harmon
Designer: Pooja Bakri Design
Production Manager: Hector Campbell

First published in 2005 by Watson-Guptill Publications,
a division of VNU Business Media, Inc.,
770 Broadway, New York, N.Y. 10003
www.wgpub.com

Library of Congress Control Number: 2005928203

First printing 2005

1 2 3 4 5 6 7 8 9 / 13 12 11 10 09 08 07 06 05

All photography by Jennifer Lévy unless
otherwise noted on page or as follows:
Page 30: Photography by Gail
Oskin/WireImage.com; Page 44:
Photography by Kent Smith/WireImage.com;
Page 72: Photography by Steve
Jennings/WireImage.com; Page 92:
Photography by Butch Dill/WireImage.com;
Page 102: Photography by Darl
Zehr/WireImage.com.

Licensed by

Acknowledgments

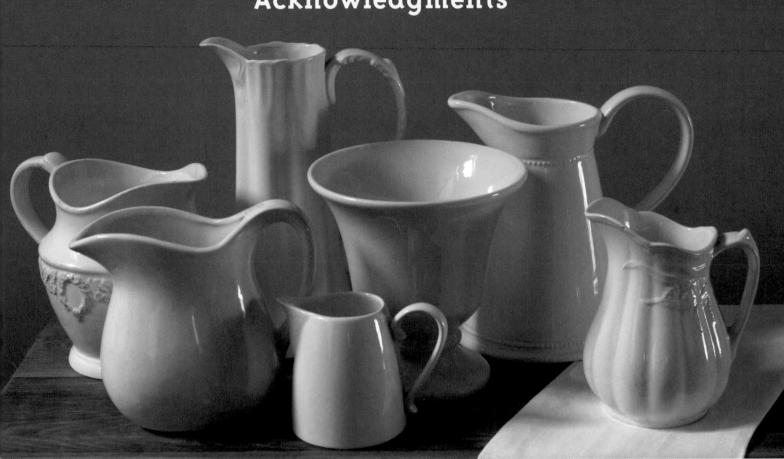

This book would never have been created without such a supportive network of people around me. Special thanks go to:

Brice Fridlington, my intern and assistant, worked tirelessly on this project, and helped construct many of the projects. She's been an amazing asset to this book.

Jennifer Lévy, my photographer, friend, and partner in crime. Her amazing talent brought my ideas to life, and I feel lucky to have been able to work with her.

Everyone who let me use their homes as backdrops: Jackie and North Peterson, Patti and Danny Kennelly, and Ann and Tom Sulivan.

Elisa Trachtman and Howard Lewis, for their unfailing kindness; and Kieran Juska, for her friendship and constant use of her Rolodex.

And last but not least, my mother and brother, for everything.

Contents

Introduction

My first eBay experience was so exceptional that eBay became an immediate part of my daily life. A few years ago, I discovered some vintage cookie molds at a yard sale. There were three of them and I bought them for 10 cents each. I had a feeling when I bought them that they were worth a bit more than that, but I had no idea if they were worth $5 or $25. I didn't think much more about it until the day I realized that I could put one up on eBay to see what amount I could actually get for it. I thought my starting bid was a bit optimistic: it was $9.99. A week later, the mold sold at auction for $122.50! Not a bad return on a 10-cent investment. And not surprisingly, I have been hooked on eBay ever since.

Even if you're just the occasional online surfer, you can't have missed the Internet auction craze. Thanks to eBay, we've become a nation of collectors. And I'm one of them. My life-long love of flea markets has been transformed into a love of e-markets. I love surfing through auctions, looking for interesting pieces that will round out my décor. Even when I'm not looking for a specific item, I'll spend hours searching eBay listings to see if there's a bargain. There are often times that I didn't know I was looking for something until I actually found it online!

Clearly, I'm not alone. Since its founding in 1995, eBay has become the world's online marketplace. With a community that stretches around the world, eBay is a contemporary phenomenon. As of this printing, eBay had a reported 147 million registered users, more than 50,000 categories, and a record number of over 400 million listings. Among those listings are millions of items for home decorating—including some pieces that you may never have considered before.

And that's where this book comes in. Both a sourcebook and idea book, *The eBay Home Makeover* is a comprehensive guide to how to decorate your home from top to bottom all through eBay. There are tips and tricks from eBay professionals, easy-to-do makeover projects, and decorating advice from an interior design pro. In addition, there is a comprehensive buyer's guide with over 140 sources to show you where to go for the best deals on eBay.

LEFT: The Internet offers a wide variety of items to satisfy even the most demanding consumer. You can find everything from vases to large furniture pieces, usually at a fraction of the cost if purchased offline.

Throughout the book, there are elements designed to offer inspiration and advice to get you started. Look for:

* do-it-yourself inspirations: These idea sections are meant to encourage you to rethink and reinvent something that may be a steal but isn't, well, high style. I give you step-by-step illustrated instructions, and tell you what tools you'll need to complete the job. These projects are super-easy and none take more than a weekend. Several cost under $100, but most come in under $50. Plus, most projects offer alternative ideas, so readers can go a step further if they desire.

* decorating tips: Interior designer Tracy Bross offers advice on virtually every decorating subject in detailed, illustrated tip sections appearing throughout the book. Tracy brings her vast experience styling homes to provide expert insights and professional tips on how to combine all your furniture and design elements into a stylish décor. From how to make a room plan to how to paint furniture, these tips will make you a savvy decorator overnight.

* dream room makeovers: From leather club chairs to lava lamps… from Persian rugs to Pottery Barn sconces… eBay's five Dream Room Contest finalists have purchased it all! Best of all, they achieved these incredible transformations in only four weeks and with a budget of only $2,500. See their rooms, read about their adventures, then check out our buyer's guide to see where you can purchase items to create your own "dream room"!

* buyer's guide: The Buyer's Guide showcases over 100 of eBay's best sources for home décor items. Many people don't realize that there are literally tons of retailers selling their merchandise through eBay every day. Each listing includes the seller's eBay ID, a detailed description of their products, plus coverage of the seller's eBay ratings and payment options—all to help you shop on eBay effectively.

Getting Started

Naturally, the number one thing you need to get started on eBay is an Internet connection. Once you have that essential, log onto eBay's home page at www.ebay.com. Now the fun really begins. . .

Buying on eBay couldn't be easier—just register, browse or search, bid or buy, and then pay. If you have any questions, visit eBay's Buy Hub. This is the main hub for all content on how to find items and to buy on eBay. Click "Buy" at the top of any eBay page.

✳ **register:** Registration is required to buy or sell on eBay. It's easy and free! Register by clicking on the Register link at the top of any eBay page. First, you will be asked for basic contact information. This information remains private on eBay's secure servers. Accept the terms and conditions (you must be 18 years or older to register), create a user ID and password, and then look for your e-mail confirmation message. Follow the instructions within the message to confirm your registration.

✳ **browse or search:** Browsing is clicking through lists of titles called Categories until you find something you're interested in. Click on individual categories to narrow your search. To search for an item, type a few keywords into the search box.

✳ **bid or buy:** When you find an item you like, simply place a Bid or Buy It Now. When you place a bid, enter the maximum amount you are willing to pay for the item. eBay will bid on your behalf only if there is a competing bidder and only to your maximum amount. When you click Buy It Now, you agree to pay the stated Buy It Now price and avoid competing for the item. Keep in mind that once you bid on an item, that bid is binding.

✳ **pay:** To see if you've won an auction, either go back to the item page, check your e-mail, or log onto My eBay. (Each member has his or her own personal My eBay page. Just click on the link on the top of any eBay page, and enter your User ID and password.) Any of these will provide you with a Pay Now link. If you selected a Buy It Now option, you will immediately be led to checkout.

Buy with Confidence

Here are a few programs to help you trade safely and enjoyably in the eBay marketplace:

Feedback: The Feedback score and rating enable people to know what other eBay members think about transactions with an eBay seller or buyer.

PayPal: Register for PayPal so you can use your credit or debit card to instantly send payment for an item. It's the safe way to pay because your financial information is not shared with the seller.

Security & Resolution Center: Want to learn how to trade safely? Visit the eBay Security & Resolution Center.

If you've never bought online before, you're about to embark on a truly exciting experience. Imagine being able to buy anything you want or need for your home—new and old furniture, knickknacks, collectibles, artwork, window treatments, rugs, decorative objects, even the house itself—without ever leaving your home. That's what eBay does for you! And, it makes it so easy.

ABOVE: Everything from furniture to textiles, fine art to flooring, can be purchased safely and securely online at eBay.
(Top: Photo Courtesy of Jazzy Decor. Bottom: Photo Courtesy of Classy Yet Affordable.)

The eBay Community

eBay is more than an online auction site. It's a worldwide community! Meet people who share your interests, get the most up-to-date eBay news, and learn more about your item's seller before making the binding bid. Visit the Community Hub for a complete list of community resources. Here are some of the ways you can take advantage of this opportunity:

Discussion Boards: There are over 80 Discussion Boards where you can go to find people who buy and sell in your categories.

Answer Center: When you have a question, you can get help from experienced eBay members at the Community Answer Center. Most questions are answered within 20 minutes!

News: Check out the Announcement Board, your official source for eBay news and updates, to learn about new eBay features, products, promotions, and more. Read *The Chatter* for stories about other members and to read articles about all-things eBay.

Community Calendar: The Community Calendar has a complete list of eBay online and offline events.

Workshops: Workshops are one-hour educational events, combining "lecture" material with interactive discussion between eBay staff and members.

eBay Groups: eBay Groups connect you with other members who share your interests. Want to meet other members in your area? Join a regional group. Need some advice? Check out a mentoring group.

Feedback: Visit the Feedback Forum to learn about your trading partners, view their reputation, and express your opinions.

Tricks of the Trade

I've been buying on eBay for a long time, and I'd like to pass on a few things I've picked up, clever tricks—insider secrets, if you will—that will help you navigate the eBay world like a pro.

Searching: Know that a lot of sellers make typos, or just can't spell, or list things in the completely wrong categories. So, in addition to searching by categories, make a keyword search (a search by the *name* of what you're looking for: "china cabinet," "area rug," or "window treatments"), so all options come up, even those mis-categorized. Try variations: "sofa" and "couch"; "blinds" and "shades." And try different spellings: looking for a chaise lounge? Try "chaise longue" or "chaze longe." And be sure to check out eBay's General Search Tips.

Sniping: Last minute bidding (or sniping) can mean the difference between winning or losing something you really, really want, and a good, fast Internet connection gives you a real advantage. If you've got a high-speed service, swoop in with the high bid at less than 60 seconds to go in the auction. The odds are very high that the other bidders won't have the time to counter-offer, and the object of your dreams is yours. (I really have to emphasize the importance of high-speed here: a DSL or cable modem connection is necessary. I lost out on a lot of great auctions because I couldn't get my bids in fast enough on my old dial-up connection.)

Buy It Now: If you absolutely love something with a Buy It Now feature, my advice is to buy it, *now.* Often the difference between the seller's asking price and the "Buy It Now" price is nominal. Isn't it worth an extra $20 to ensure you'll get that McCoy vase you've always wanted? Who can put a price tag on love?

EBAY GLOSSARY

Bid: Placing a monetary offer on an item up for auction.

Bidder: The person placing the bid on the item up for auction.

Buy It Now: A preset, fixed price on a listed item that allows you to buy the item outright for the Buy It Now price, rather than waiting and bidding for it at auction.

Buyer: The person who won the auction and will buy the item.

Category Listing: The way all items for sale on eBay are organized. You can search for items by browsing individual categories or subcategories. (You'll find furniture, for example, in the Home and Garden category.)

Contact Information: This is the information you provide about yourself when you register at eBay: your name, address, phone number, etc. You can request contact information for other eBay users only when you are involved in a current or very recent transaction with them as a bidder or seller.

eBay Stores: Virtual stores on eBay where sellers "set up shop" and offer all items they have for sale in one place. (Many sellers offer items from a variety of categories and subcategories. Their eBay store is the one place all those items can be viewed together. See the eBay Buyer's Guide in the back of this book for profiles of leading eBay Home Stores.)

Featured Listing: Special areas of eBay where items get prominent highlighted coverage: Featured Plus listings, Home Page Featured listings, and Gallery Featured listings.

Feedback: Comments and ratings by users about their experiences trading with one another. Feedback is posted for every seller (and buyer) for whom comments have been made. Click on the "Feedback Forum" link on the eBay navigation bar for more information about ratings and feedback.

Gallery: An eBay special feature where a small, thumbnail picture of the item for sale appears alongside that item's listing in the category list. Pictures are provided as JPEG files by the sellers.

High Bidder: The buyer with the highest bid and auction winner.

Keywords: Words you use to search for items.

Live Help: eBay's real-time, chat-format Customer Support. This works like instant messaging, where you type your questions into a dialog box and an eBay Customer Support person writes back immediately with answers and information. To utilize Live Help, click on the "Live Help" icon.

Live Auctions: A way to let you participate, in real-time, in auctions at some of the most famous auction houses. These auctions are really taking place in brick-and-mortar settings, with auctioneers, and bidding audiences.

MIB: Abbreviation used by sellers to identify items that are "Mint in Box," meaning items in their original packaging, in pristine condition, or those items that were never opened and removed from their original packaging.

Minimum Bid: Seller's designation of the lowest possible initial bid that can be made on an item.

My eBay: A page to help you keep track of all your eBay activities: buying, selling, watching, tracking, or purchasing. This page cannot be viewed by anyone but you and can help you keep track of favorite categories, review current bidding activities, check your account balance, and let you know feedback about you.

Navigation Bar: A graphic bar at the top of every eBay page with links to every part of eBay. The best place to start a search or get an answer to any question is with the navigation bar.

Outbid: When another bidder has placed a higher maximum bid than yours. If you are outbid, you will be notified via e-mail.

PayPal: An online payment service that enables buyers to instantly send secure payment to sellers using a credit/debit card or bank account.

Power Seller: An eBay ranking for sellers whose sales levels and extremely high customer satisfaction ratings qualify them as among the most successful on eBay. Look for the "Power Seller" logo in the item descriptions and in eBay Store locations.

Proxy Bidding: An automatic bidding system. When you bid on an item, you enter the maximum amount you're willing to pay for it. This amount is kept confidential. As other bids for that item come in, the eBay proxy system keeps placing bids on your behalf, using only the amount needed to maintain your high bid position.

Registered User: Designation that allows you to buy and sell on eBay. To become a Registered User, click the "Register Now" button on the Home Page and fill out the form.

Regional Listings: Items listed according to geography.

Reserve Price: A specific, hidden price, below which the seller will not sell the item.

OPPOSITE: **Create a welcoming entryway with attractive and comfortable carpets and richly colored walls.**

Searches: How to look for items you're interested in buying. There are six types of searches: Title Search, Advance Search, Search by Item Number, Search by Seller, Search by Bidder, Search Stores, and Search Completed Items.

Secure Server: A special server connection used for sensitive and/or confidential information like credit card numbers. eBay's secure server transmits your data over the Internet in a special, secret encryption so that no outsider can steal your information.

Seller: The person selling the item.

Sniping: Bidding in the last minutes or seconds of an auction.

Starting Price: The price at which bidding begins for an item (see also Minimum Bid).

User Agreement: The terms of use for eBay service that all registered users must agree to before they can bid on or list items, or use any other eBay service.

User ID: A unique nickname you choose when you register at eBay. Everyone on eBay has one, buyers and sellers alike.

CHAPTER

1

WINDOWS & WALLS

Layers of sheer curtains and swags in a variety of hues bathe a room in a rainbow of glowing color.

THE EBAY HOME MAKEOVER

Restyle for Less

You can transform the look of an entire room easily and affordably with fresh window and wall treatments. Whether you're starting with bare windows and walls or sprucing up an existing scheme, eBay offers a treasure trove of decorating ideas to suit any taste and style. On the following pages, you'll find some great tricks and tips from eBay pros to help you find what you need, as well as some fun projects to bring new life to secondhand classics.

Window Shopping

Windows are often the focal point of a room, and as such, they deserve star treatment. Lavish them with stunning designs that combine good looks with practicality. On eBay, you can find curtains, drapes, blinds, and shades to go with every personality and decorating scheme. In addition, there is a wide assortment of materials that—with a little creativity—can be transformed into beautiful custom window treatments.

CURTAINS & DRAPES

On any given day, you can find over 5,000 listings for curtains and drapes on eBay. In addition to secondhand treasures, there are tons of great deals on branded items. Some popular brands buyers often look for in this category include Pottery Barn, Ikea, Croscill, and Waverly. As an alternative, you can explore the antique and collectible categories for vintage treasures.

In addition to curtains and drapes in everyday fabrics like cotton and polyester, you can find styles in an assortment of luxurious materials. Use keywords in your searches to find a desired fabric, like dupioni, silk, velvet, and satin. There are even drapes in rich jacquard and damask fabrics as well. When shopping for particular patterns or styles, try using an asterisk in your search to find variations of a keyword. For example, typing "check*" in the search box will return results with patterns described as check, checked, checkered, or checks in the title.

Click into the categories to find standard drapery lengths, such as 63 inches for windowsill length, or 84 inches for floor. (To determine the proper curtain length for your window, measure from the top of the rod to the desired bottom point.) Some sellers on eBay even offer the option of custom drapery that can be designed to specifically fit a buyer's windows.

When choosing curtains, look for colors that match or blend with the tones of the other furnishings in the room. If the perfect color isn't available, you can use fabric dye to custom-color a purchased curtain or drape. For a polished look, consider adding tiebacks, swags, and jabots to your window design.

In addition to the drapery panels themselves, there are curtain rods, hardware, and other accessories for windows available on eBay. Sometimes little details like finials and tiebacks add just the right finishing touch to a treatment.

Shades can be as plain or elaborate as desired to blend with any setting. Made in white cotton, this simple fabric shade lends privacy to the room while bathing it in a softly diffused light.

BLINDS & SHADES

Window blinds and shades add a dimension of color and pattern to a room while solving a variety of window dilemmas. With their compact design, shades and blinds are the perfect solution for hard-to-fit areas where traditional curtains or drapes would be impractical or impossible. Simple fabric curtains or shades can adapt easily to any decorating scheme. Depending on the fabric chosen, they are equally at home in the kitchen, living room, or bedroom. Because they raise and lower easily, shades are ideal for rooms that require privacy and light control.

Material is an important factor when considering blinds. When searching eBay for blinds, be careful to distinguish between faux wood listings and real wood listings. If you want to exclude faux wood, use a minus sign to structure your search (for example, "Wood -Faux"). Try to narrow the listings to the specific style you're looking for, using keywords for different types of blinds and shades, such as roller shades, Roman shades, cellular shades, honeycomb shades, wood blinds, or mini blinds. Look for unique styles that can't be found in your average store, like Japanese bamboo, matchstick shades, or rice paper and shoji blinds.

✳ Hanky Sheer Curtain

Not very long ago, women carried handkerchiefs in their handbags. Both of my grandmothers had large collections of them, many with beautiful lacework and monograms. The hankies were passed on to my mother, who still carries them instead of tissues. I, too, have my own cache, but because they're heirlooms, I'm always afraid that using them will ruin them. When I came up with the idea for this project, I immediately started looking to buy them on eBay. They had to be affordable, and easy to come by. Imagine my surprise the first time I searched for the word "hanky" and more than 2800 active auctions came up! Buying what I needed was simple and fast, and I had everything in hand in a matter of days. (You might want to buy a few extras, just in case, because you never know how they'll look together till you lay the hankies out next to one another.)

The thing I love most about this panel is just how fragile and sheer it is. It doesn't obscure the light—it enhances it. The subtle and delicate stitches come alive, and a dozen simple handkerchiefs become a one-of-a-kind, custom curtain in under an hour.

How to buy them: Buying hankies in "lots" is cost-effective. Sellers tend to sell more detailed hankies solo, and they cost more. So buying several at a time can get you a lot for your money. Know the buzzwords: handkerchief linen and hand-rolled edges mean exactly what they say. Better hankies are made of linen. Either cotton or linen can be used for this project.

How to care for them: Vintage linens often come yellowed, but they're relatively easy to restore and care for. Handwash in either an oxygen-based powder detergent, or a detergent booster like Biz. Never, ever use chlorine bleach. To do: fill a dishpan with very hot water and as much detergent as the box says for a full load. Drop the linens in, and stir. The water will get dirty quickly, so rinse and repeat till the water stays clear. It may take a few hours, or a few days, but it's perfectly safe to leave them soaking until the stains are gone.

1

Choose hankies that are similar in size and color. I chose white-on-white as my color scheme so that I could use ones that were either lace-trimmed or embroidered.

2

Lay out the hankies to create a mock-up of your sheer. Move them around until you find the right mix: mine was three hankies across, and four down.

3

Sew the hankies together at both the corners and middles, with thread matching the colors of the fabric. A few stitches in each place are all you need to tack the sheer together.

LEFT: eBay's Wall Décor category includes everything from Asian fans and ceramic tiles to tapestries and shadow boxes. Try shopping according to various style words, such as shabby chic, country, Asian, contemporary, or use thematic words such as nautical, hearts, or stars to find products that revolve around the particular theme you're using in a room.

RIGHT: Purchased murals and simple paint effects can be used to create artistic wall displays. Look in the Crafts category for stencils, paint, and brushes if you would like to create your own design, and under Murals and Wallpaper Cutouts for easy to do, yet creative ideas.

Wonderful Walls

Want to transform your plain walls into works of art, without draining your savings account in the process? Why not embellish them with wallpaper or paper borders, or add decorative flourishes like tiles and tapestries? With just a small investment, you can give your walls a winning style. Even little details like outlet covers can add personality to a room. At this book's printing, there were over 7,000 outlet covers to choose from on eBay.

LEFT: An allover floral wallcovering adds comfort without formality. This richly patterned setting features traditionally styled floral wallpaper played against coordinating curtains and rich wood floors and furnishings.

RIGHT: Borders are a simple way to dress up walls when you don't want to cover the whole wall in paper but would like to introduce a pattern or print.

Wallpaper & Borders

Depending upon the style, wallpapers and borders can make anything from a casual to an elegant statement. There are a wide variety of papers to be found on eBay in an assortment of colors and patterns. Everything from textured and metallic papers to toile and vintage patterns can be easily found. Search under the style word to find the ideal wallcovering for your room. If you don't want to cover an entire wall, look for an attractive paper border to add dimension or a splash of color and pattern to a décor.

If you're decorating a specific room, such as a kitchen or bathroom, try searching under the room name (kitchen, bath, or bathroom) to view wallpaper selections sellers have specifically called out for these rooms. Use the category structure to narrow listings down to the type of paper you're looking for, such as borders, murals, rolls and sheets, or wallpaper cutouts.

Choosing Color

Often, all it takes is a little added color to make a wall sing with style. For inspiration, check resource guides in the back of design magazines to find what colors the designers used in their rooms. You can also take pictures and fabric swatches to the paint store and find matching paint chips. Then, take note of the brand name and color that you like.

Look in the Crafts category to find stencils, stamps, and other creative tools you can use to add a dash of color and design to a room. If you are painting an entire room, buy pint cans of various colors to test on the wall first if possible. Try to do it on a white wall in an even light, and make sure you paint two coats.

You can use color to highlight details and architectural features. Contrasting colors on moldings and architectural elements can add definition to a space, and is a good method for adding color to a room where you don't want to put too much on the walls. Bear in mind that whatever color is on the walls, white ceilings and white trim is a classic look.

Whether painting or wallpapering a room, dare to be bold in your color selection. Don't rule out dark colors because you think it will make the room feel smaller. Dark colors can make the room more cozy, rich, and dramatic, and you'll find the room looks just as big. And keeping every surface gleaming white (perhaps mixing paint finishes) is a stunning way to go, too.

PAINT: WHAT YOU CHOOSE CAN MAKE—OR BREAK—THE ROOM

Paint color can perform many functions in a room, from making a powerful statement in and of itself, to serving as the barely noticed background to your furniture, art, and accessories. Here are a few basic color schemes:

Warm & Neutral: Is your furniture upholstered in bright fabrics or big prints? Do you have a lot of decorative objects on display? Are your accessories bold and eye-catching? Is your artwork a dominant focal point? If you answer yes to any or all of these questions, it's best to paint your walls with warm, neutral paint colors (just about any shade of white, for example), which will unify disparate pieces and provide a backdrop that won't compete with what you want people to notice.

ABOVE: Here, neutral furnishings make the bright, splashy color scheme possible.

Bold: Are your decorative objects all in the same color family? Is your artwork in monotones or black-and-white? Is your furniture in pale or neutral fabrics? If this describes your décor, bolder, deeper wall colors will add interest and make your neutral or monochromatic pieces more lively and interesting. They will also emphasize the size and lines of your pieces.

Contrast: Are architectural features your fancy? Does your room have distinctive design details? You can emphasize the unique detailing in your own home with a creative approach to painted moldings, fireplaces, and window and trim work. Contrasting colors, complementary finishes, even paint effects, can all bring out the special features of your room and make them a noticeable part of your décor.

Tone-on-Tone: Have you considered tone-on-tone? A room whose furniture, art, accessories, and wall color are all one tone looks very clean and sophisticated. In my apartment, I've used five shades of white paint to echo and emphasize my all-white decorating theme: white pottery, white linens, white upholstery, white painted furniture, white rugs, and white accessories. You can also create variety by using the same paint color in several different finishes: eggshell on the walls, semi-gloss on the trim, and high-gloss on the mantle, or, by painting or stenciling designs on walls, the floor, or funiture in the same color, but with a contrasting finish.

Rack It Up

The vintage pressed-glass knobs I used to create this "peg" rack are all the rage right now. Large retailers who specialize in reproductions sell glass knobs and pulls in all shapes, sizes, and colors—not unlike the real, vintage items you can find online.

The difference? The real McCoy usually sports more facets and detailing in the glass. This extra detailing was at one point essential as it hid any defects or marks in the glass-pressing process. Consequently, original vintage glasswork has more depth and sparkle than reproduction glass. Prices vary, but I found antique knobs at auction starting at $2.99 each. Try buying them in sets, for bigger savings. (For a unique look, search for several different kinds of knobs to mix together.)

I chose simple, clear knobs, but there are lots of choices out there. Sheer colors include green, blue, pink, or amber. Opaque milk-glass, named for its milky appearance, comes in shades of blue (sometimes known as Delphite), green (or Jadeite), or traditional white. Another choice would be Vaseline glass, which looks very much like frosted glass.

If you're interested in learning more about vintage glassware and collecting glass hardware, you'll find all the information and products you need online. A great, historic place to start is the site for the famed Corning Museum of Glass: www.cmog.org.

How to buy glass hardware: Search for both "knobs" and "pulls," as both will yield results. Read descriptions carefully; a lot of sellers say they're selling "vintage style" hardware, which means they're selling new reproductions. Be sure the knobs you buy come with their own hardware, otherwise you'll have to hit your hardware store to find compatible nuts and bolts. Ask sellers questions: are the knobs chipped or cracked in any way? These flaws might get you less expensive pieces, but when buying used glass be sure to err on the side of caution: make sure it's perfect.

How to care for them: Soak hardware in warm, soapy water—a regular dish soap is all you need. If needed, use an old, soft-bristle toothbrush to clean in hard to reach areas. Rinse well, then dry knobs with a lint-free cloth and polish till they shine. When installing hardware, be careful when tightening the bolts: too tight and you can shatter the glass.

How to use them: Using knobs like these in places other than this rack—like your kitchen or bathroom—will give rooms an instant retro makeover.

You'll need a board for the base (I turned a plain board into a faux-weathered one with crackle-paint), three glass knobs and their hardware, and a drill.

②

Mark where the knobs should go, then drill holes for their hardware. (Note: Always wear safety glasses when using power tools!)

③

Once the holes are drilled, attach the hardware. When you're finished, hang the board as desired.

Dream Room Makeover

**For my tastes, eBay is just extraordinary.
It allows me to find genuine,
handmade items from around the world.**

Tressa Carrier

When you've traveled the world, it's hard not to want to bring a bit of the world back home with you. That's exactly what eBay user Tressa Carrier set out to do. With less than $2,500, Tressa transformed her once barren bedroom into an exotic yet serene retreat. Her bedroom now reminds her of the hotel rooms she has stayed in while traveling on business in Europe, India, and China. "It's tranquil, yet elegant, and a little offbeat," says Carrier of her new room. "I would call it contemporary ethnic."

Having just bought her first home, Tressa found that the one space that needed remodeling the most was the master bedroom. Now, thanks to the eBay Dream Room Contest, Tressa's room features international touches at every turn, from a Tibetan elm cabinet and antique Chinese table to an iron Moroccan chandelier and a pair of Persian rugs. Chinese and Thai wood panels accent the walls, while an antique mirror fitted with Indian mango wood increases the exotic atmosphere.

Five lucky finalists in eBay's Dream Room Contest earned the opportunity to redecorate a room in their homes with $2,500 to spend on eBay. This is the first of those rooms you'll see throughout this book.

Items Purchased on eBay by User ID: assertc

Fire Flower-Carved Teak Wood Panel—Thailand Art
$68.90
Unique Moroccan Hand Crafted Ceiling Iron Chandelier
$109.98
9 Switchplates: Asian Bali Scrolls
$81.00
King Size Euro Swerved Platform Bed & Two Night Stands
$500.00
9'3x6'6 Mashad Persian Rug
$245.52
Tibetan Old Painted Elm Wood Low Cabinet
$197.14
Chinese Antique Carved Small 1-Drawer Table
$173.25
12'8x9'7 Mashad Persian Rug
$440.00
Arabian Paisley Ottoman Set
$475.00
Taj Archway Mirror—Indian Antiqued Mango Wood Art
$97.95
India Vintage Textile Label Oleograph Peacock
$5.00

Total Spent $2,393.74

CHAPTER

2

FLOORING &
LIGHTING

Comfort Makers

The best rooms are always the ones that combine comfort, purpose, and style. Nothing adds function and flair to a home's interior as much as its flooring and lighting. Every day on eBay there's an incredible variety of designs and styles of rugs and carpets, lamps and wall fixtures to choose from that will suit every decorating need and desire. In addition to some practical advice on finding the items that you need, I've included some illuminating ideas on how to transform ordinary objects into extraordinary lamps. Sometimes the best ideas are right under your nose!

OPPOSITE: An attractive area carpet over a wood paneled floor is a classic way of creating an intimate setting.

ABOVE: Natural fiber flooring and metal sconces on paneled walls lend to the cozy, cottage feel of this home's décor. Wicker chairs, a collection of botanical still lifes, and a stone fireplace enhance the overall charm.

Beauty Underfoot

No matter if bare wood or soft carpet, nothing announces a room like a floor. In fact, a room's floor can often dictate the entire decorating scheme. So, it's a good idea to choose your flooring before you plan your décor. On eBay, you can find everything from brand new tiles and wood floors to antique and imported rugs. Expect to be floored by the choices.

Tiles are an ideal choice for high-traffic areas like kitchens and halls. In addition to laminate, you can choose from cool stone, soft leather, and even cork and concrete.

FLOORING

Select flooring that complements the size and design of your home (if you need help, many eBay sellers provide excellent customer service). To get started, you can browse the category structure by material types, including marble, wood, granite, ceramic, and laminate. You can also try typing in geographic regions to find imported products, such as Mexican tile. There are also some unique decorating options to choose from, such as floor medallions and mosaics.

Many sellers offer beautiful brand-new flooring at a price by the square foot. Simply order the quantity of square feet you need. Others offer minimum shipments of a full pallet. Be sure to read the detailed item description to understand exactly how each seller has made the floor available.

CARPETS & RUGS

Area rugs and carpets are always comfy underfoot, and are a great way to add color and pattern to a room. In addition to traditional Oriental rugs, eBay offers lots of hard-to-find styles such as sisal, seagrass, faux fur, and braided rugs. Use the Rugs Finder on eBay to identify characteristics you like, such as age, shape, size, style, and background color. Be sure to check Shipping Costs so that you can calculate the total cost of your purchase. (If you'd like to add a column to see shipping costs for all listings, click the Customize link under Search Options on the left side of the page.)

There's no place like home. . . the rich colors and patterns of a Persian carpet make even the barest room feel warm and comfy. (Photo by Gail Oskin/WireImage.com)

Set matching floor lamps next to chairs and couches to provide light for reading and other seated activities.

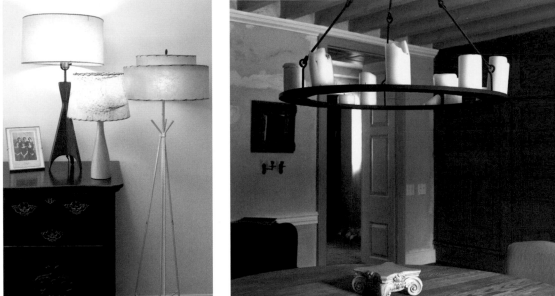

LEFT: With stylish shades and clever bases, these lamps do much more than shed light. Vintage table and floor lamps add personality and a sense of style to any room.

RIGHT: You can find gorgeous nonelectric cast iron chandeliers like the one pictured here by narrowing your chandelier search with the words Cast Iron, Antique, and Vintage. This chandelier can also be hung from a porch ceiling for an outdoor seating area.

In a New Light

On any given day, you'll find a large selection of lampshade and lamp options on eBay, ranging from sconces and chandeliers to table and floor lamps. In addition to brand-new items, there's a wide assortment of vintage styles to choose from. And eBay has recently added new categories for pendant lighting and recessed lighting to meet the increasing volume of listings. (Pendant lighting has become very trendy above kitchen islands and dining tables.)

To narrow your search, try typing style words, such as Tiffany, Mission, Retro, Victorian, or Rustic to view a smaller selection that fits the style of your room. If you're looking for sconces, bear in mind that there are multiple locations you should check out if you want to view the full selection. There is a Sconce category under Wall Décor, another under Candles in Home Décor, and a third under Lamps, Lighting, Ceiling Fans.

Choose lights that both practically and decoratively meet your needs. And keep in mind that you can easily dress up a plain or battered fixture with a new shade or a little paint and fabric. Often all it takes is a little creativity to transform a bargain into a shining star.

✱

Beaded Lampshade

I always look for ways to combine materials that wouldn't, on the face of it, seem to go together. Here, the intricate, shimmery metallic beading from a vintage evening gown—handiwork that, nowadays, would cost thousands of dollars!—turns a simple bedside lamp into a luxe accent piece.

This type of adaptive reuse was difficult until eBay came along; it would have been a matter of pure serendipity to find a gown like this in a secondhand clothing store. And while I have a huge garment bag's worth of my grandmother's ornate gowns stored in my Mom's attic, I'd hate to cut them up. That's another great reason to buy them on eBay.

If you're seeking beadwork like this, know that it, more often than not, comes on a separate piece of fabric from the garment it's attached to. Presumably, the beadwork and dress could be made in different places, then assembled at the designer's warehouse or showroom.

How to buy beading:

To find beads on eBay, include a variety of relevant keywords in your search, such as beadwork, vintage, or women's clothing. Look for pieces that come apart from the garment they're attached to. That will make for neater edges, and give you less to worry about. Be sure to have the seller affirm that the beadwork is still tight and that none of the beads are missing. For metallic beads, ask whether silvery pieces are shedding. (Metallic beads are made similarly to mirrors; glass, with metallic paint on the back. As they age, the paint can sometimes chip away, making the piece lose shimmer.) Ask about shipping costs beforehand; beadwork can be quite heavy, and you should know the exact price from the get-go.

How to care for them:

While it's likely that beaded sections could be handwashed, I wouldn't recommend it. If you feel you need to clean the one you have, bring it to your dry cleaner to make sure it's done safely. Otherwise, use a blow dryer on a no-heat setting to blow away any dust.

How to display them:

If this lamp project is a little flashy for you, beaded sections make for great art all by themselves. Shadow-boxes are the best way to display beads without crushing them.

①

With a seam ripper, remove the beaded panel from the rest of the dress fabric. It's often easier to cut out the whole beaded section, as I did, so there is less excess fabric.

②

Place the beaded fabric around the lampshade to decide how to position the beadwork. I had two matching pieces and wanted to be sure I could fit both on the same shade.

③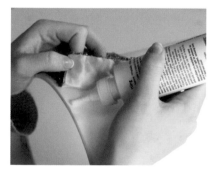

Attach the beading onto the lampshade with strong-tack fabric glue. Be sure to let it dry fully while the shade is still on it's side. The beading is heavy, so you want to make sure the glue dries thoroughly before turning the shade upright.

Luminaria Alternatives

The word luminaria, which comes from the Spanish for "lamp," usually conjures up images of sand-weighted paper bags with designs pricked through them, a soft glow emanating from inside. Customarily, they're placed along the sides of a path at Christmastime, or for vigils and certain religious or spiritual ceremonies. With a little creativity, though, the luminaria can be reimagined in a variety of fun ways.

Vintage mason jars fill my home—some hold staples in my pantry, some work as vases, while others house a button collection—so envisioning them as luminaria was a no-brainer for me. The jars are unbelievably affordable, and come in both clear and blue hues.

The idea for the ladle came as I was gathering up my kitchenware for another project. As it hung near my stove, I immediately envisioned a candle sitting in the well.

When I tried to come up with new ways to turn retro items into lanterns, eggcups came to mind. I chose the ones with the chicken pattern because they're one of my favorite "finds." But I think they would have looked equally nice placed in a Fire King Jadeite egg-cup. (Auctions for these restaurant-ware items start around $10.)

Finally, the graters. They're so much fun, and I just adore them. Kitchen items like this can cost a mere 50 cents. . .look at what that spare change will buy you.

How to buy luminaria alternatives: Each one of these has different criteria: ceramic eggcups should be without chips or cracked glaze; mason jars should be wide mouthed with working hardware; graters should sit sturdy without wobbling; ladles need a good place to hang.

How to care for them: Wash after each use to remove smoke stains and wax residue.

A few caveats: Luminarias get really, really hot. Always burn them on a fireproof surface. Even after you've blown out the flame, make sure they cool down all the way before picking them up. And keep them out of the reach of children and pets, for obvious reasons.

CLOCKWISE FROM TOP LEFT: Mason jars are my favorite luminaria to light. Whenever I have a party, I line my long hallway with them, placing them next to the baseboard. Such a great mood for an intimate gathering.

The well of this shabby chic enamel ladle serves as a resting place for a simple candle.

The openings in these rusty, rustic box-graters let a candle's glow shine through. I chose larger candles to sit inside, to make sure they gave off enough light for the grater's size.

Cute, country eggcups make for curious luminaria. Like the others, I simply dropped in a couple of votive candles.

Dream Room Makeover

You can shop at 2 p.m. or 2 a.m. and often the seller's descriptions have more information than what you would find at a retail store. eBay is really in a class by itself.

Tami Hechtel

Inspired by author Hane Ray's story *The Twelve Dancing Princesses,* eBay user Tami Hechtel transformed her five- and three-year-old daughters' bedroom into a fanciful royal chamber. The room is now bright, whimsical, and elegant, not to mention full of secrets and surprises—perfectly befitting Tami's two little princesses!

Originally boring white, the room's walls were faux-finished in rose and salmon and then accented with swirls of gold. The old ceiling fan was replaced with a vintage chandelier with petal-covered shades. Colorful bedding, creative bedpost coronets, fanciful sun and moon wall masks, and flower-shaped shelving further add to the room's fairytale appeal. There is even a gowned princess mannequin whose train is slightly suspended to reveal a secret play area! And every special something was purchased on eBay.

Items Purchased on eBay by User ID: theartfullife

Custom Deluxe Twin Bed Set-Skirt, Duvet, Pillows, etc.
$1,600.00
Mirrors—Baroque Wall, Mirror with Cherubs
$23.90
Fanciful Frogs Horny Toad New M/B
$33.99
3-Inch Wide Gesso Brush
$3.99
1 Quart Acrylic Gesso
$9.99
Vintage Shabby Magazine Rack Table Chic
$63.00
2 pair size 9 shoes Pumps Heels Dress Shoes Lot No Res
$23.28
Bookends—Elegant Ivory Finish Scroll Bookends
$88.00
Sconces—(2) Scallop Wall Sconce Shelves
$96.39
Twin White Goose Down Feather Comforter 40 oz
$47.99
Vintage Metallic Gold/Coral Renaissance Costume Gown
$88.00
Schonbek Petite 5 Arm Brass & Crystal Chandelier
$106.00
Old Set of Venetian Drawers
$18.55

Total Spent $2,203.08

CHAPTER

3

FURNITURE

Moving the Immovable

If you're looking for furniture, you really don't need to look further than eBay. Whatever your needs, whatever your taste, you'll find it there, among the thousands of furniture items listed every day. Looking for a Victorian settee? You'll find it. A steamer trunk? Dozens. A coffee table that matches your dining room set? It's there. And, while there is a wide selection of older pieces, over 70 percent of the furniture is brand new! These items are often sold at a great discount over what you could get in a traditional retail store. You can find everything from an Ikea bookcase for $1 to a $19,000 complete set of Ethan Allen furniture.

If the thought of buying furniture online is daunting to you, you're not alone. I, too, was very wary before I bought my first large piece, an antique bed. I had a lot of questions and worries: How long would it take me to find what I wanted? How many options would I have? How would I know what it really looked like? How could I tell if it was in good condition? Would I be able to have it shipped to me? Was it safe to give my money to someone I'd never met before? Despite my worries, once I actually started looking at things on eBay, I realized there wasn't anything to worry about at all.

So, how can you buy something so substantial, virtually sight unseen, and get what you paid for? Easy—take the time to examine your online purchase the same way you'd examine one from a brick-and-mortar store. Virtually all online sellers provide photographs of what they sell, usually from several different views, including close-ups. Written descriptions are usually quite detailed, and information about measurements, weight, and shipping options is provided, too. But since you can't actually touch it, sit on it, or walk around it, you're going to have to ask the seller a lot of questions beyond what you see in the listing.

Here are a few of the questions you may find yourself asking:

If you're looking for wood furniture: Is the piece solid or veneer? Are there scratches or dings in the wood? Is there any chipping or splitting of the veneer? Would you please take close-up shots of the problem areas and e-mail them to me?

If it's a piece like a dresser: How are the drawers constructed? Do they open easily? What's the hardware made of? Is it intact? Is it rusty? Is it original? Does the piece itself wobble? Does the seller know the history of the piece?

If you are looking at upholstery: What's the fabric content? Is it Scotch guarded? Are there any tears, rips, or stains? What's inside the cushions? Are the springs intact? If you're looking at leather furniture, ask: Has the leather aged well? Is it cracking?

What it comes down to is this: Ask. Just ask. That's the best advice I can give you for buying furniture online.

Don't let fear of the unknown keep you offline shopping for larger items. If you do your homework, you can purchase every item shown in this room online—and with complete confidence.

TREASURE HUNTING

Are you on the lookout for old and unusual furniture pieces to add vintage beauty to your home? Shopping on eBay is one of the best ways to get the most for your money, and you can do it from the comfort of your own home. The key to successful antique shopping is discovering the gems hidden amidst the rubble. Items that some see as worthless reveal a wealth of creative potential to an informed and practiced eye. On the following pages you'll find information to help you discover and choose the best buys, as well as some ideas for transforming your finds into unique home accent pieces. Here are few tips to help you get started. Happy hunting!

• Browse in home décor magazines and catalogs for ideas and inspiration. When you find a piece you like, note the words that are used to describe a particular piece or style (for example, French club chair or Chippendale chair); then, use similar words to start your search on eBay.

• Read the item description carefully. Note the condition of the piece and pay close attention to detailed photographs that the seller provides. (If the listing is light on pictures and you are serious about the piece, you can ask the seller to send you additional photographs.) Be sure to note if the item is new or used, an original antique or contemporary reproduction.

• Measure twice, shop once! Before you start looking for furniture, note the dimensions of the space you need to fill and measure your doorways and/or windows. Keep those measurements close at hand when you're shopping. When you find a piece you like, check the dimensions closely to make sure it will fit in the space you have in mind for it. If exact dimensions aren't detailed in the listing, e-mail the seller and ask him or her to provide them.

• Check the seller's shipping costs and terms. (See page 51, for more on Shipping Solutions.)

• Find a seller you like? Add him or her to your favorites and get updates whenever they list new items. Click on the "Add to Favorite Sellers" in the Seller Information box at the top of the listing page.

Children's Furniture

On eBay, there's a whole category dedicated specifically to Children's Furniture. You'll find many branded items, such as Pottery Barn Kids, as well as nonbranded items, old and new. Looking for bunk beds? On any given day, there are over 350 different styles of bunk beds to choose from on eBay. (Type "bunk*" to find all the variations of bunk bed listings.) You will also find items to furnish an entire nursery, from cribs to changing tables and toy chests. There are lots of good storage solutions for playthings as well.

Mixmatched items can be painted to appear as if they are all of the same set. Ideal for a children's room, this bench opens to reveal lots of extra storage space for toys and blankets. (Photo by Butch Dill/WireImage.com)

SHIPPING SOLUTIONS

You can often save on shipping costs by buying multiple items from the same seller and combining them into one shipment. To view other items from the same seller, either click on "View Seller's Other Items" or check out their eBay store. Here are some other tips on shipping to help you shop savvy:

Distinct and elegant, this dining room set reflects the tasteful expression of the entire room. The rich, dark finish of the wood pieces stands out against the pale yellow walls and upholstery.

Check with the seller first: Many sellers have already worked out shipping costs and methods. Sometimes the shipping is free, sometimes a figure is stated in the listing, and sometimes you have to calculate the costs yourself after getting details from the seller. Some sellers ship directly and others use third parties to ship for them. Be aware that shipping via the vendor won't always be the cheapest method, so you'll have to do some research. If you do find a better, cheaper way to ship, be sure to ask the seller if that's an option before you bid. Also ask where the vendor is located. If you're within driving distance, picking it up yourself is ultimately the cheapest way. (You can easily search for items on eBay that are located within a given radius of your home: click on "Advanced Search" at the top right corner, then scroll down and request "Show Only" items within a certain distance of your zip code or city.)

There are basically three ways to ship: 1) Sellers pack and ship themselves, via carriers like UPS, Fed Ex, and trucking companies. **2**) Sellers use a packing and shipping service such as The UPS Store, where the item is delivered to the service location. The service then packs it and ships it for a fee above the actual UPS shipping fee. **3**) Finally, there are online service companies (such as FreightQuote.com, available at http://ebay.freightquote.com) that can do most of the work for you, even arrange for a shipper/carrier to go to the seller's home, pick up your item, pack it, and then ship it to you.

Do your homework: All shipping carriers have different weight and measurement guidelines, and what one company won't ship, another will, happily. (When I bought my bed, I called a ton of shippers. All of the companies except one, Airborne Express, refused to handle a package like mine.) Be sure to know these details about your item before you look for rates from shippers: dimensions (length, width, depth); weight; special packing needs (glass tabletops, delicate legs, detailed edges, extra tall, etc.); and insurance information.

Redecorating an entire home? Just make your plan, then go shopping: From the color scheme to the patterns, everything in this living room is well-matched.

Mixing Furniture Styles

1. Express your taste and personal style: I've found that one of the most effective ways to achieve a striking and personal room is to mix different styles of furniture. It's a sure way to avoid the cookie-cutter look that furniture "sets" can all too easily present.

2. Start with furniture you love: Furniture pieces of different styles and from different eras can always be mixed together, especially when they are distinctive pieces you really love.

3. Combine textures and materials: When mixing styles of furniture don't be afraid to mix textures and materials, too. Using different types of wood together, such as a mélange of rattans, oaks, maples, mahoganies, and even lacquers, or mixing natural elements, such as copper, brass, and steel with various woods, can define the look you are going for. Similar finishes, all matte, or all glossy, can also pull the look together.

4. Keep it simple: When you combine different furniture styles together it's better to stick to basic silhouettes and shapes. Look for pieces that are the most simple, or pared-down version of the individual styles or eras.

5. Use fabrics and accessories to unify the look: Upholstering pieces in the same fabric can bring a common thread throughout any room filled with a mixture of styles. When selecting accessories such as window treatments, pillows, and rugs, pull colors and patterns from the upholstery fabric, or, keep them all neutral.

6. Set the theme: It's sometimes easier to achieve a big impact by anchoring a room with a few simple, similar pieces, and then spice it up with a peppering of smaller, bold furniture pieces and accessories.

7. Strive for compatibility of style: Be consistent in mixing styles from room to room, particularly in rooms that flow into one another, such as the dining alcove off the living room, or the family room that flows from the kitchen. Keep a bit of the same eclectic mix in all rooms.

Makeover Magic

The real joy of searching through secondhand items is figuring out which nothings can be turned into somethings. With a little ingenuity, you can turn almost any toad into a prince. The trick is to train your eye to recognize obscure objects with the potential for greatness. Look for unusual items at bargain prices that you can transform into fun, functional, and good-looking home furnishings.

Certainly if you're after high design, you won't want to reimagine Grandma's old ironing board as a sideboard. But if a little kitsch is just the thing, it's easy to turn some off-the-beaten-path items into conversation pieces. In addition to reinventing an old ironing board and ladder, I have spruced up some uninspired furniture pieces with a little imagination and some decorative paints. Follow the step-by-step directions, or use them to inspire your own magical makeovers.

DECORATING TIPS WITH TRACY BROSS

Painting Furniture

1. Select the right paint for the job: Indoor and outdoor painting methods vary, depending on the piece, the look you want, and where it will live. Outdoor furniture requires paint that can withstand the elements; outdoor deck paint works well and is easy to clean. Water-based paints are good for interior furniture, and come in a range of finishes from flat to high-gloss. The glossier the finish, the easier it is to clean.

2. Analyze surfaces and textures: Make sure the surface of your piece can handle at least a light sanding, to give some texture for the new paint to adhere to. Some wood veneers are quite thin, so sand these lightly and with care. Formica and plastic furniture need an oil-base paint for a consistent and even finish. (Have some paint thinner on hand to mix with your paint if it gets gloppy.) Wood pieces that are stained and sealed need to be sanded until the shiny finish is gone in order for the paint to adhere.

3. Always test before starting the job: Always test samples of your different paint and color options first. You won't know exactly how the paint will work on your surface until you try it. Test paint for wood or metal furniture on the bottom or inside of the piece; different types of woods and metals take paint differently. (It's even better if you can find scrap wood or metal that's similar to what you're painting for your test.)

4. Proper preparation will save you big headaches later: Either remove the hardware or tape over it so that you don't get paint on it. Take caution with hinges and gliders because drips of paint can impair their function. Cover the floor area with an inexpensive plastic drop cloth or old shower curtains. If you're using spray paint or oil-base paint, make sure there is good ventilation in the room. Oil-base paints don't clean up with soap and water like water-base paints do, so make sure you're covered properly.

5. How to get a distressed look: Sometimes just sanding off some of the existing paint can create a great vintage or distressed look. Rotten Stone is a product that can also give a distressed look; just mix it with water and apply it to the painted or sanded surface. For a heavily distressed, aged look, bang up the piece with an old bike chain to make small nicks in it and then wash over with the Rotten Stone.

6. Make sure the surface you create will clean and wear well: When painting something white or any light color, consider putting a sealer on it or a more glossy finish so finger prints clean easy. The sealer might also protect it from water marks and other spills, as well as scratches.

7. Adding details: Stencil kits are a great way to add detail and dimension to a painted piece. Try monogramming a chest of drawers or a wood-framed mirror. Faux finishes on drawer fronts dress up a piece as do faux paneling details on doors. Marbleizing the top of a piece, then putting on a shiny sealer, can also be a great look if the real thing is not an option.

Painted Sidetable

This decorative painting idea was inspired by hand-painted furniture I saw while on vacation in Provence. I'd picked up a few French design magazines, and as I was flipping through them, I saw several pieces decorated this way. The idea was so unique and interesting, I immediately knew I wanted a piece of furniture just like it.

To that end, I decided my first try at this one-of-a-kind design approach would be on an affordable side table. While I chose a side table, dressers, breakfronts, armoires, or buffets are all good furniture choices for this paint treatment.

Don't worry too much about making your piece look perfect; the homespun charm is a large part of the appeal. I painted this table freehand, in about an hour. I chose the lines quoted from a favorite poem: T. S. Eliot's "The Love Song of J. Alfred Prufrock."

How to use decorative paint: For this project, I used colorful craft paint. You can buy it at craft and hobby stores—though I've found some great deals for it online—and it comes in a rainbow of colors. Each jar costs a few dollars, and it's acrylic, so your paintbrushes are washed easily with soapy water. I recommend plain, animal hair paintbrushes, because they hold just the right amount of paint and provide for a softer stroke. Some people squeeze craft paint onto a surface, like a plate, and dip their brush in that. I'm pretty low-maintenance about projects like this, and I'm just as happy to dip my brush in the bottle.

How to choose colors: I wanted some bold and brilliant colors for this project, so I chose pinks and purples. For a subtler piece, you can use three colors (including the main color of the piece) that are all in pale, more neutral colors. Those colors would lend a more romantic, softer feel than the bold one I've created.

(1) Give your piece of furniture a base coat of semi-gloss latex. Choose a plain color, knowing that the adorning will be done with the painted poem.

(2) With a pencil, write out the poem you've chosen, then use decorative acrylic craft paint to paint your poem in a whimsical color. Choose other coordinating colors for border designs or free-form flowers.

✳

Stereo Cabinet

The following two makeovers are exceedingly simple, requiring nothing more elaborate than a quick sanding and a few coats of paint. They're meant to inspire you to look past an offbeat paint job and see how an item can be transformed. Finding pieces that you can reinvigorate or repurpose is easy—starting prices on eBay for armoires and wardrobes are often under $20, and you can surely find something you like that won't cost a lot.

This cabinet, which sits in my living room, was once a child's wardrobe, complete with yellow baby chicks painted on the front. As soon as I saw it, I knew it had good bones: the shape was good and the piece solid. There were numerous sturdy shelves inside, and it was trimmed in egg-and-dart molding, which I love. If I hadn't seen beyond the oddly handpainted baby birds, I'd have passed on this piece. Painting furniture is something you should approach thoughtfully, but when done right, it can really transform a piece without a lot of effort.

How to Paint Furniture

My brother used to joke that I was going to be sent to "wood abuser's prison" for painting perfectly good wood. Truth is, I like painted furniture. And some pieces, like this wardrobe, do better with a few coats of new paint instead of stripping off the old.

Start by lightly washing the piece with a mild cleanser, to remove dirt. Once dry, give the piece a quick sanding to provide for both an even and paintable surface. After sanding, wipe down thoroughly with a tack cloth to remove all residue.

Semi-gloss enamel is the paint of choice; it offers protection from stains, yet since it's water-based, it's easy to apply. Paint your piece with several thin coats, letting it dry well in between each.

Wait several days before placing anything on top of a newly painted surface. The paint needs to be really dry or things will stick to it and ruin the new surface.

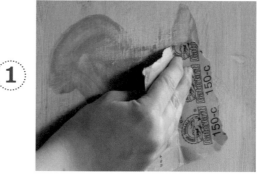

① With a little medium-grit sandpaper, I smoothed out the raised pattern.

② Then, I painted the surface using a small roller brush and three coats of paint.

This simple, elegant cabinet does more than hold your entertainment system—
it addresses the Mars/Venus conflict about where stereo systems should go.
(Your husband wants yours displayed like a trophy; you want it out of sight.)

OPPOSITE: Before foregoing an online buy that doesn't seem right for you, imagine what a simple coat of paint could do.

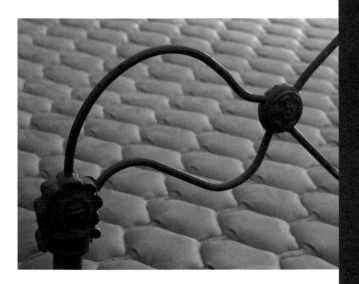

1 A quick sanding roughened up the surface enough for it to be paintable. No need to sand off all the paint; that's far too much work!

2 Finally, the paint. I used a latex enamel, which holds up pretty well. A small paintbrush helped me get into the nooks and crannies. I used the same brush to paint two coats of white onto the bed. It was dry in less than an hour.

DO-IT-YOURSELF INSPIRATION

The Painted Bed

I had been looking for a bed like this, especially one with a footboard, since I was a little girl. I searched estate sales and garage sales and antique stores, and came up empty. The few times I found one I liked, it was far too expensive to buy. Enter online auctions.

It came from a farmhouse in Ohio. The previous owners had called it "Uncle Louie's Red Bed." The story was that their Uncle Louie had had a rather racy girlfriend, and she painted his bed—this bed—red. He'd left his furniture to his nieces, and they were liquidating the pieces online.

Red is not for me, and although most of us don't know it, these types of antique metal beds can be easily painted with latex enamel, nothing special needed. In a couple of hours, my dream of a vintage white metal bed was fulfilled. I dressed it in my favorite retro linens, and was ready to climb in for an afternoon nap. Sweet dreams.

What to look for: Make sure to ask a lot of questions before buying anything online, especially something this substantial. Many antique beds come without side rails—which you'll need—so be sure to double-check. Get the measurements, too—lots of these old beds came in a size larger than a twin but smaller than a standard double. If you buy one of those, you'll need to use specially made sheets. . . what a hassle! Note also that Queen-sized beds weren't available at the time these beds were originally made, so the only way you'll find one is if it's been refurbished.

How to get it there: Shipping large furniture is never easy, but there are some tricks to help. The best scenario is finding an auction piece that you can pick up yourself. Since this isn't always an option, do your homework. There are lots of shippers out there, and each have different requirements for what they will ship, and to where. Call for estimates. Places like The UPS store will pack and ship things to you if your buyer can bring them there. Finally, there are companies that will pack and ship the items to you. Check with your auction site to see what they recommend.

Memory Dressing Table

What little girl doesn't want her own dressing table? They're perfect for sitting down in front of and scribbling in your diary; and just the place to sit and apply the first dabs of make-up while getting ready for your first date.

I always wanted a vanity table when I was a little girl—feel free to tell my mother, I'm sure I have at least once!—and this project gave me the opportunity to make a one-of-a-kind version for my friend Crissa's two nieces. Crissa has had this table sitting in her mother's basement since we were children, and asked if I could do something with it. I asked what colors the girls liked, and she told me that pink was an absolute must. I knew the finished product would be perfect for this book.

eBay is filled with lots of dressing tables, many needing a fun makeover like I did here. Because you'll first be giving the piece a facelift with a coat of paint, the condition of the table doesn't matter. Just be sure the legs aren't wobbly, and that the top is sturdy.

If decoupage isn't your thing, another great idea is to get a piece of glass cut to the shape of the table. Underneath, you can place mementos like pictures, ticket stubs, invitations, or newspaper articles. Use your imagination!

How to decoupage: The dictionary defines decoupage as "the technique of decorating a surface with cutouts, as of paper." That pretty much says it all, and you'll be surprised at how easy this craft is. If you can cut on the lines and glue, you're in business.

I used preprinted decorative paper, made solely for this purpose. It gave me lots of patterns to choose from, and enough material to cover a large area.

You don't need to follow this example, however. There are many things to decoupage with. For other projects, I've used vintage stamps, photographs, magazine cutouts, and more.

My favorite decoupage medium is Mod Podge. It's thick and covers well, but doesn't sink into the paper and make it buckle.

(1) Clean the table with a damp rag and wipe it dry. Begin by painting the table with two coats of semi-gloss latex enamel, letting dry between each coat. I chose this pink color to complement the colors in the flowers I decoupaged.

2

Using small scissors—or an X-acto blade and a cutting mat—carefully cut out the designs you want to adorn your piece with.

 3

Apply a water-based decoupage medium, such as Mod Podge, to the back of each flower, then press firmly in place.

4

After all the flowers are arranged, use a larger paintbrush to cover the entire surface with the same glue. It will work as a sealant, protecting the flowers.

5

I love using small touches for a more finished-looking piece—like wallpapering the inside of drawers.

*Ironing Board Sideboard

What's so great about using an ironing board as a sideboard? First, it is a genuinely unique way to show off what was once a castaway piece of household goods. Plus, as a home décor item, it immediately invokes curiosity and nostalgia. It will remind everyone of the days before sending clothes to the dry cleaners was de rigeur. I chose to polish mine to show off the beauty of the wood, but like so many of the projects in this book, it has a myriad of finished surface possibilities.

Why an ironing board? Well, they're easy to come by—after all, all of our grandmothers had one. Plus, they're super-sturdy, perfect for use as a sideboard, buffet surface, or bar.

What to look for: Make sure the one you purchase is solid, not wobbly, and stands flat on the ground. Some come with wrought iron legs, others with wooden ones. If the board is in good shape, it's a matter of preference and how well it matches your décor.

Keeping it in good shape: No matter how sturdy, it's best not lean on this piece of furniture, or have it hold heavy objects, like books. Keeping it in great shape involves regular dusting, and rewaxing every few months or so as needed.

Start by removing the board cover and the padding—once I started peeling these back, I found layer upon layer of old padding in between several of those old heat-resistant fabric covers.

Once I washed off the surface—a good, oiled furniture soap works wonders—I let it dry and then smoothed out rough edges with a small electric hand-sander.

Instead of varnishing the board, I used paste furniture wax to give the wood more depth of color, and to protect its surface. Simply rub the paste on with a rag, let dry, then buff off with a clean rag.

✳

Ladder Magazine Rack

Rickety wooden ladders are a staple in the back of most people's basements. (Most were forgotten when aluminum ones came into the picture.) While old wooden varieties are usually not safe enough to support any real weight, they've become a trusted, shabby-chic style accessory, for use as either a magazine or towel rack. I chose the former, and decided to leave our ladder as "authentic" as possible, simply sanding down rough patches. Still, I've seen these ladders haphazardly painted to look even more distressed, or, painted perfectly, complete with floral designs. Choose what works best with your style and décor. Another ladder redo option is to pull apart the ladder and use just the front half, with the rungs. (Most ladders you see in décor magazines are done this way.)

How to determine whether your wood is worth repair: Check that nails and bolts are tight and not sticking out. Does it feel wobbly, like the glue is coming undone? Look at the surface for cracks or termite damage. Press on it; does it give way? Splinter? If not, it's likely sturdy enough to continue.

How to care for it: Dust regularly. If you can't get into tight spots, use your vacuum cleaner's crevice attachment. As mentioned in the how-to steps, you may also wash it with a safe-for-wood cleanser.

①

Damp paper towels or rags were all we used to clean the ladder. Special wood soaps (like Murphy's Oil) help clean wood without drying it out.

②

A small hand-sander was used to smooth out rough and splintered areas.

Space Planning 101

1. Determine the overall environment you want: Minimal, clean, and simple or cozy and cluttered? Have a vision and a plan when you begin. I like an eclectic mix of furniture, but I do subscribe to the less-is-more rule, too. I also tear out lots of pictures of rooms I like from magazines, then use them for inspiration.

2. Make test furniture layouts before you start moving furniture: Take the length, width, and/or depth measurements of each furniture piece. Without moving furniture, tape out these measurements on the floor with masking tape to see exactly where the furniture will sit in the room. You can also create a scaled rendering of the room itself on graph paper by measuring and marking the length of each wall, door opening, window placement, etc. Furniture shapes are also easy to scale on graph paper; just scale the furniture measurements, plot on the graph paper, cut them out, and arrange them on your scaled floor plan.

3. Begin the plan by selecting the essential pieces: Decide on the basic pieces, the ones you absolutely need for the room to function, and be practical. Then, based on your budget, your first investment(s) should be for the essential pieces you don't currently have. You can always add accent pieces later. Here are a few basic room plans that will work in most spaces and for an array of lifestyles: Living room: Sofa, 2 chairs, coffee table, 2 end tables, and a pair of lamps. Dining room: Table and chairs for 4–6, sideboard, and lighting. Bedroom: Bed, bedside tables, lamps, and a dresser.

4. Traffic patterns matter as much as the furniture pieces: When laying out your furniture, be sure to consider how people walk into and through the room. Remember to leave adequate space for opening doors, cabinets, and drawers, and to allow access to all electrical needs for lighting and electronics. Doors need 36" of swing space, and dining chairs need about 24" to move in and out. For easy traffic flow, place furniture pieces 30"–36" apart, or 36" from the wall. Coffee tables should sit 18" from the sofa.

5. Use the whole room, not just the walls: Avoid lining everything flush up against the room's walls; moving the furniture even 6"–8" away from the walls creates the illusion of more space and provides a visual border. Create different environments by grouping together things that function and/or look good together. To create a conversation/social area, place two chairs or sofas facing each other along with a cocktail table and side tables and lamps; to provide a practical reading environment (as well as the visual interest of varying heights), group a chair, ottoman, standing lamp, and side table.

6. How to position furniture around and over rugs: When using area rugs in a space, make sure the furniture sits either all on the rug or all off the rug. Otherwise legs will wobble and pieces will tilt. Visually, it's pleasing to see an 18"–24" wood, tile, linoleum, or carpet border around the area rug. If you want to cover up an ugly floor, buy an area rug that will cover the floor to within 2" of the walls; it will look and feel like wall-to-wall carpet. When selecting rugs to place on top of wall-to-wall carpet, stick to flat-weave rugs like a Kilim or Dhurrie because they aren't too thick and bulky.

7. With measurements, the third time's the charm: Double- and triple-check all your measurements of the room and the pieces you're bringing in. When measuring the room, make sure to take note of alcoves, bump-outs, corners, fireplace hearths, floor and ceiling moldings, and beams. And, for stress-free delivery, don't forget to measure exterior doors, hallways, stairs, and elevators.

When planning a furniture layout, consider traffic patterns as well as common usage. Leave space for people to walk through the room, with lots of leg room in front of chairs and sofas.

DO-IT-YOURSELF INSPIRATION

✳ Storage Solutions

Unless you live in a huge house with enormous closets, there's one thing each of us always needs more of: good storage. And nothing's better than storage solutions that look really attractive, like these four varieties of cleverly stacked tables.

Alone, each piece is a storage container. Piled together, they become small- to medium-sized tables that add a lovely touch to any room—from the retro feel generated by the woven, striped suitcases, to the warm, homey aura of the wicker picnic hampers. Suitcases and wicker picnic hampers are great to use, because they come in all shapes and sizes (and the wicker color turns more rich and golden as they age). Wooden wine and liquor boxes are an unexpected and unique touch, and they, too, age beautifully. And the printed tin picnic hampers—the ones that look like wicker but aren't—are reminiscent of the kind your grandmother always used for summer potlucks.

When it comes to creating stacked tables, anything goes. Pile them high or low, angle them to fit in an awkward space, use several as a TV stand (suitcases are good for this), or group several stacks together to create a one-of-a-kind coffee table.

Just be sure the containers can handle their own weight (especially with the wicker hampers), as well as the weight of what you both put in them and on top of them. Use your common sense: If you choose to stack them high, do so against a wall, so they won't fall over. Keep them out of your child's room or reach, because little fingers can easily get caught, and the stacks could fall if a child tried to climb them.

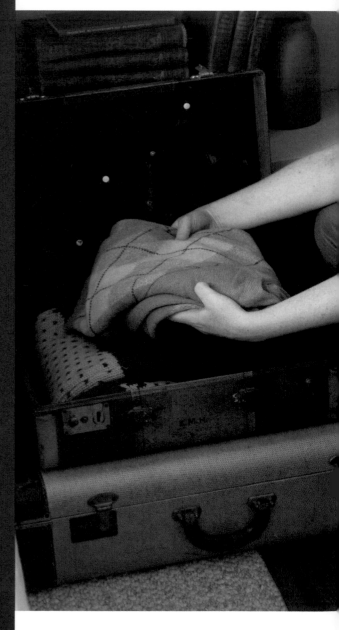

When these suitcases aren't being a table, they're perfect for storing winter woolens because their tight, fitted closings keep air and pests away. To be on the safe side, I toss in some cedar blocks or mothballs along with the woolens.

All of the stacked tables pictured here belong to me, and, not surprisingly, there are a lot more where they came from—one might say, "boatloads more." Because I have a lot of stuff to store (clothes, fabric, linens, kitchenware, more clothes, more fabric, more linens, more kitchenware. . . I'm sure you get the gist), I am always looking for attractive ways to stow it all away neatly. These stacked tables have been the answer to my storage problems and could be for yours. You just need to find the right case or hamper for the job and follow some simple care rules that will help them last a lifetime.

How to care for suitcases: If yours needs a good washing, it's best to do it outside with the garden hose, a scrubby sponge, and mild soap. Let it dry in the sun. Let the suitcase air for a while to help keep musty odors away.

How to care for tin hampers: To clean, use mild soap—dishwashing liquid is a good choice—and wash with a soft, nonabrasive sponge or cloth. Hand-dry thoroughly with a dry, soft fabric cloth to keep hamper from rusting. Avoid spray cleansers as they can damage the printed patterns.

How to care for wicker hampers: Wicker can be washed, in the tub or outside, with a mild wood soap, such as Murphy's Oil Soap. Gingerly use a soft scrub brush to loosen dirt or debris. Rinse off, and then leave in the sun to dry.

How to care for wooden wine crates: Before stowing anything inside them, use medium-grade sandpaper to sand down any rough edges, inside and out. Look for any loose nails or tacks and hammer them firmly into place.

Think these are woven wicker? Look closer: they're actually vintage tin picnic hampers, printed with the pattern of wicker. Since they're all the same size, they stack beautifully, and because they're airtight, they protect the stored items from air and dust. But since they're lightweight, be sure to fill them before stacking so that they don't topple over.

When it comes to storage solutions, you'll find nearly a thousand different choices on eBay. Search for a unique armoire to enclose a TV, or consider a storage ottoman (look for ottomans in the Footstools category, located under Living Room Furniture).

ABOVE: Because they're unfinished, rustic-looking wood, these wine and liquor crates are perfect for outdoor storage of things like outdoor pillows and accessories. Even better, since they're available free from your liquor store, you don't have to worry about them being rained on.

LEFT: Wicker picnic hampers let air (and dust!) flow through, so they're not the best for storing clothes. Use them to store items, like books and magazines, or anything that's easy to dust off.

Dream Room Makeover

On eBay, you never know what you might stumble upon. You can follow threads and end up learning (or finding) something really unique that you hadn't even realized was out there.

Maerian Morris

University assistant by day, swashbuckling romantic by night—that's eBay user Maerian Morris. And Maerian's dream living room is as unique and interesting as she is. Reflecting her passions for period sailing, fencing, and 16th- through 19th-century history, Maerian decorated her living room with warm leather chairs and solid-oak Mission-style furniture, amber and stained-glass Tiffany lamps, an assortment of nautical knickknacks, and an exotic Persian rug.

Even before becoming one of the finalists in eBay's Dream Room Contest, Maerian had been enjoying shopping on eBay for years. Besides the convenience and selection the marketplace offers, she loves eBay because it makes shopping fun and interesting. To her, eBay's rich, diverse community is the key. "eBay has many faces," she says. "I would rather deal with a vast and eclectic bunch of people from all over than a faceless corporation."

eBay Search Tip

Decorating around a theme can really help unify a room. If you're trying to achieve a nautical theme, try typing some of these words in the search box: nautical, ship, sextant, maritime, scrimshaw, and galleon.

Items Purchased on eBay by User ID: maerian

Pair of Vintage Pirate Ship Galleon Wall Plaques
$27.26
Bill Blass Faux Fur Throw Blanket Comforter, Silver Wolf
$75.95
Dale Tiffany "Renaissance Revival" Table Lamp
$94.71
Club Chair Ottoman Leather Furniture Chairs
$849.00
Nautical Large Sextant with Mahogany Box
$41.90
KPSI 140 Very Fine 7x10 Persian Mashad Rug
$359.00
Tiffany Golden Amber Floor Lamp
$89.99
Mission Frank Lloyd Wright Style Stained Glass Lamp
$54.90
Solid Oak Mission Night Stand End Table—New
$109.00
H.M.S. Bounty Stained Glass Walnut Frame
$353.44
American Arts & Crafts Small Footstool c1900
$219.34
Vintage Windsor Wheel-Back Morris-Style Chair
$225.00

Total Spent $2,499.49

CHAPTER

4

TEXTILES

Rags to Riches

Fabrics are among my favorite things to collect. So it was no surprise to anyone when I began selling linens, textiles, and lace on eBay. These were the early days of eBay, when there weren't huge amounts of linens sold online, and prices for those that were went sky-high. I once sold a child's handkerchief for $42 and a fleur-de-lis patterned damask tablecloth for over $100. Sadly for me the seller, those days are gone. But happily for me the buyer, there are now so many fabrics, linens, and lace up for sale or auction at any given time that the prices have been driven way down. It couldn't be a better time to buy fabrics and linens online.

Nowadays, eBay is an inexpensive and satisfying way to buy both vintage and new fabric items. Sheets, napkins, pillowcases, hand towels... all are for sale in mass quantities. Vintage linens are especially ripe for the picking. Old linen bed sheets, tablecloths, and napkins were made to last, and are especially appealing if they bear embroidery that resonates with days past. Likewise, old curtains can be altered into slipcovers, pillows, and bedcovers. Napkins and tablecloths are also popular, as are old dishtowels. Even lace tablecloths can be reinvented as bed coverings.

The key is to think imaginatively. It doesn't take a magic wand to transform an old tablecloth

Vintage linens are charming, practical, and plentiful. Instead of looking for matching sets, mix-and-match colors and patterns to spice up a table setting. Old tea cloths and dishtowels can make colorful, oversized dinner and picnic napkins.

into an attractive window shade, or to turn an embroidered handkerchief into the perfect pillow top—all that's needed is a little creativity. If the fabric has a stain or tear, don't let that deter you. See if there is enough usable fabric to make a pillowcase or chair cushion. I am not suggesting cutting up priceless antiques, but instead I am encouraging you to find innovative ways to rescue and recycle vintage household textiles and give them new life.

In home decorating, the traditional and handmade is in. Pieces of our heritage are now welcome parts of our present day décor. By mixing and matching vintage and newer textiles in your fabric furnishing, you will give your home an irresistible sense of whimsy and originality, combined with a hint of nostalgia.

I hope you have as much fun exploring all the wonderful fabrics and textiles on eBay as I do.

The e-fabric Question:

With so many linens up for sale, how do you begin? Well, there are two ways: Search eBay, or, navigate eBay categories. If you're just browsing, the navigating approach is great, because the travel through all the categories lets you "window shop" until you find something you like. If you know exactly what you're looking for—a hanky with an "M" monogram, for example—eBay's search feature will direct you to all the "M" monogrammed hankies up for auction.

Search for the same item under several different names. Some sellers will say "handkerchief," some "hanky," some "hankie" and some even "kerchief," so search all the possible variations and alternative spellings. Tea towels are also known as "hand towels," "dishtowels," and often, a seller not completely familiar with linens will call them "placemats." Quilts are also called "patchwork," and curtains will also be called "valances," "drapes," or "drapery."

SEARCHING AND NAVIGATING FOR FABRIC

To search eBay, go to the eBay Home Page (http://eBay.com) and find "Search" in the upper left of the page, under the "Find" heading. Type in your search word (for example, "fabric" or "linens"), and click the "Search" button.

To navigate eBay's Textile category for vintage linens, for example, start on the Home Page, in the upper left, under the heading "Browse for an Item." Click on the arrow, scroll down the list, select "Antiques," then click "Go."

Selecting Fabrics

1. Make fabric a priority: Fabric is as important as furniture in creating a room's look. I generally prefer a solid for all the main upholstered pieces, then bring in the large-scale pattern as the main accent. If I need a third or fourth pattern, I will choose a small plaid that blends with all other fabric choices, and maybe another solid of one of the colors in the larger print.

2. Pick the main or featured fabric first: If you are overwhelmed by fabric choices, try to choose one main fabric that has a pattern and multiple colors, then coordinate additional ones that are simpler.

3. Make sure the fiber content is compatible with the planned use: Pay attention to what the material is made of, for cleaning and maintenance. If you are doing cotton slipcovers, wash the fabric first to preshrink it and soften it up. It's not a bad idea to pretreat the fabric with a stain guard, too. If the piece is already upholstered, you can have a professional service come and spray it with a stain guard.

4. How to (and not to) mix prints and patterns: Try not to mix too many large-scaled prints in one place. Pair them with a check or stripe that shares one or two colors with the larger print, and with solid colors that also appear in the prints, checks, and stripes.

5. Select fabrics that work well in your climate: Choose fabrics that make sense in the climate you live in: linens and cottons for summer and warm climates; velvets and corduroys for winters and cold climates. If you are in a multi-climate area mix some lightweight fabrics with cozier ones. Cotton velvet, ultrasuede, corduroy, and denims wear well and are good for pieces that get a lot of rough use (like from kids).

6. Repurposed textiles can make fabulous decorator fabric: Sheets, scarves, antique shawls and tablecloths, and saris make great fabrics for a one-of-a-kind look on pillows, bench seats, and window treatments, or draped over chairs and sofas as throws.

7. Seasonal fabric change can give you two completely different rooms in one: Make seasonal slipcovers for upholstered pieces, and change them with the seasons. A corduroy sofa could have a fresh, clean spring/summer slipcover in a floral linen, and a solid cotton chair can get cozy in wool plaid for the winter. I love the idea of upholstering all the furniture in muslin, then making different slipcovers that can be changed for seasons and/or special occasions.

Look for fabric that will match the pattern on an existing pillow or slipcover, then fashion new pillows from it. Here, an assortment of pretty floral remnants became a garden of throw pillows for a sofa.

Nothing cozies up a couch like a profusion of fluffy pillows. This plain Jane sofa has become a real eye-catcher due to a pile of colorful pillows in solids and patterns.

BUYING FABRIC SIGHT UNSEEN

When buying any item sight unseen, remember that eBay's feedback system is a great way to check the quality of a seller's products. Read the detailed comments left by other buyers who have purchased from a seller to see if anyone has made either positive or negative comments. Here are some more tips to help you shop wisely:

Know what you're buying: Ask the seller about the fabric content, the age of the fabric, and for fabric-care information. When buying vintage pieces, ask the seller whether the fabric really is vintage, or just looks like it is. If the seller isn't sure, pass. Ask the seller how accurately the color, weave, and texture of the fabric is conveyed in the photographs, and whether the fabric has a nap, or directionality. If there is a design or pattern, ask about how often the design/pattern repeats. Check on whether you can order more fabric later, or whether the piece is a one-off.

Go for laundered or dry-cleaned pieces: When you buy textiles that are not new or prepackaged (especially with linens, quilts, curtains, and throws) it's better if the fabric has been washed or dry-cleaned by the seller. Ask whether there are any spots or stains on the item and about any special care the fabric may require. Many sellers sell pieces "as is," leaving the buyer responsible for the cleaning. While this may save you some money, unless you're a stain removal guru, it can be risky.

Buy the right kind of fabric for the use: It's important to buy the appropriate fabric for the job at hand. You can't reupholster a sofa with a repurposed tablecloth and expect it to last more than a couple of months. Upholstery fabric is thicker, heavier, and sturdier than bed and table linens, curtains, and apparel fabric, and comes in wider widths: 54"–60" and wider. For textiles used in curtains, consider how sheer or opaque the fabric is, whether it will drape and flow or have body and structure, how well it will block light, and whether it should be lined to protect it from sun-fading. When it comes to bed linens and slipcovers, remember to select fabrics that will feel good against the skin. And of course table linens should be easy to launder and should hold up well through many cleanings.

Ask how the fabric has been stored: Folding fabric can leave creases that are hard to remove, especially since it's often not safe to iron vintage fabrics on high-heat settings; folding can also weaken the fabric threads over time. So, it's better to buy fabric that's been rolled up on a bolt. Plastic-coated fabrics and oil cloth should only be bought if they're rolled, because just the littlest bit of heat when they're folded will leave permanent creases impossible to get out.

Pillows & Slipcovers

Often all it takes is a new fabric cover and some decorative throw pillows to totally revamp an old armchair or sofa. In addition to the wide assortment of brand-name items available daily on eBay, you can easily fashion your own slipcovers and pillow covers from old blankets and other cloths for a truly original look.

A decorative pillow sells on eBay every fifteen seconds. You can find pillows under the Home Décor category. Click on the links on the left-hand side of the page to narrow down the selection by dominant color, pattern, or material. Or, try shopping by style or theme words, such as shabby chic, rustic, romantic, modern, African, Asian, animals, sports, or tropical. For a larger number of results, include a variety of relevant keywords in your search. For example, expand tropical to jungle, palm trees, ocean, fish, beach, sun.

CLOCKWISE FROM TOP LEFT: An antique linen cloth makes an attractive slip-cover for a wooden chair back. Simply hem the edges and add ribbon ties to secure the side edges. Make a set of matching covers to unify an odd collection of chairs.

Here, a simple chenille bedspread turns into an instant slipcover. Simply center the spread over a favorite chair, and then tuck it behind the back, sides, and around the cushions and arms until it sits smoothly.

This pillow came from what was once half of a Beacon-style blanket. (It might have actually been an authentic Beacon blanket, but the half I bought didn't have the label!)

Pillow Makeovers

Even though it's old fashioned, my mother—and I, sometimes, in really hot weather—carry around handkerchiefs instead of tissues. We both have vast collections, but tend to use only the more utilitarian ones for fear of ruining a beautiful heirloom. Some are so precious that I like to display them—I consider them fabric art!

One of the best ways I've found to show off a treasured hanky is to sew it directly onto a pillow. This morning-glory patterned hanky is a hands-down favorite in my ever-growing collection. I love its rich colors and I adore the scalloped edges; it was just too pretty to keep in a drawer. This project takes less than 15 minutes, yet has a huge impact on your décor.

If you weren't lucky enough to inherit a cache of hankies, they're easy to come by online: thousands are auctioned off every week. The patterns run the gamut: florals, vacation spot themes, hobby themes, children's versions. . .you name it, you'll likely find it. Happily, these hankies are really inexpensive (prices start under $5). And the best thing about them is that there are so many to choose from.

Hanky Pillow

To make: Wash hanky then press with a warm iron. Center hanky on chosen pillow; pin into place. With matching thread, hand sew edges of hanky to pillow. Don't make stitches too tight, or your hanky will buckle.

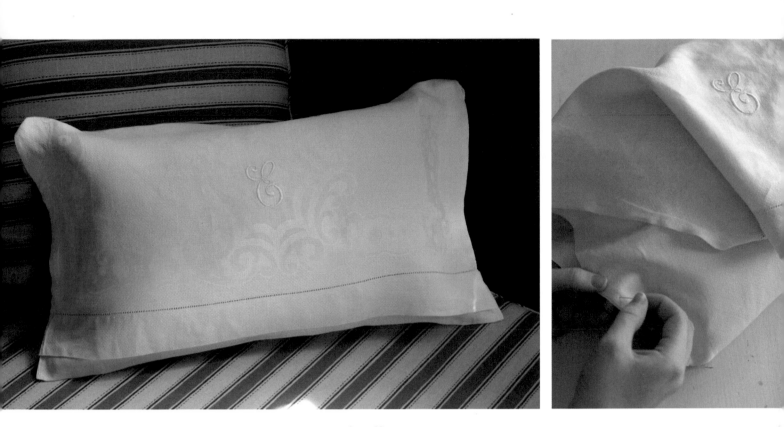

Tea Towel Pillows

To turn a tea towel into an envelope pillow sham like the one above, press the towel flat, then fold it like an envelope. Fold each long side in toward the middle, press the fold, then fold the bottom three-quarters of the way up over the folded sides. Stitch all the way up the sides to seam the edges. Slide the pillow form in at the top opening, then fold the top down to create a flap.

Simple Fabric Swaps

Fabric remnants and pieces make great pillow covers. To do this, cut the fabric to the size of the pillow, leaving 1" on each side for the seam allowance. Pin the right sides of fabric together, then sew the seams 1" in from the edge on three of sides. Turn the fabric right side out through the unsewn edge. Slip the pillow in, then blind-stitch the open edge to finish.

1

I started this project looking for interesting monograms, collecting them from eBay, estate sales, my Mom's dresser, and a variety of other sources. I then cut each one out, leaving room on all sides for selvage.

Like a puzzle, I patched the monograms together. I used a thick neutral fabric, and folded and played around with each monogram until I felt it was in the right place. I pinned them down as I went along.

A running stitch was all I needed to sew the "patches" in place and the edges under. When finished, I tacked it onto the top of a similarly sized pillow, but it could just as easily have been hung or framed.

Monogram Patchwork

I have always loved monograms. Since I'm also a lover of patchwork quilts, I was looking for a way to create a hand-sewn piece out of a myriad of monograms. Someday, I hope to have enough pieces to make an entire quilt. Till then, a pillow will have to do.

One thing I tried not to do was use my own monogram; I like to keep the ones I have for my own personal use: trimming linens or towels, creating lingerie bags.

Monograms have been along since Greek and Roman times, and until not that long ago, they were all sewn very neatly by hand. Girls learned this skill the same way they learned cross-stich and basic sewing.

In the late 1950s, the first electric monogram sewing machines were invented in Japan. Since then, it's been possible to get nearly everything monogrammed.

I prefer the handmade versions, hands-down. They're never perfect, and sometimes the stitches are crooked. But I know they were sewn with love, and that's what matters.

How to piece fabric together:
I attacked this project the way I tend to tackle things: backwards. Luckily, I'm a pretty good improvisor. If you"re not as brave—or, possibly, as stupid—as I am, I'd suggest cutting each monogram into same-sized squares and sewing those together the same way you would if you were making a real patchwork quilt.

How to sew them: Call me old fashioned, I think that hand-sewn quilts look a lot better than those done on machines. They have a homespun look that keeps each one unique. Since few of us have the kind of time it takes to hand-quilt, most modern patchworks are made on machines. Still, I chose to sew this pillow by hand. Why? The vintage fabrics were fragile—especially the ones made of handkerchief linen—and I wanted to be sure none got caught in the machine and snagged. Plus, since the project took such a short time anyway, I wanted to be sure I used the age-old techniques.

✱

Retro Tablecloth Projects

I don't know why these wonderful retro tableclothes went out of style. . .They're colorful, whimsical, and just plain pretty. I love them, and have a pile I cherish and use all the time. They're certainly easy enough to come by: searching eBay for the words "vintage, printed tablecloth," yields several hundred auctions, most of which are offering cloths in the $10 range. Not bad for tablecloths that only a few years ago sold for several times that, at the very least.

When I was selling linens on eBay, I'd regularly sell table-cloths like these for $50-$100. But sellers like me flooded the market. Hence, the prices went way down—much, much less than what you'll pay even in antique stores. Use this to your advantage when looking for linens for these projects; you don't have to spend a lot to get a lot.

The most coveted cloths to find? Those from the '40s that are printed with state maps. They're lots of fun, with artwork depicting cities and landmarks.

Other prize cloths include any with bold Mexican-themed patterns, most of which were created to complement Fiestaware and its many colorful knock offs.

How to buy tablecloths: Read the auction descriptions to find out the fabric. Most of these cloths are woven cotton, with the thickness of canvas but very, very soft. Ask about stains, rips, or tears—vintage items are rarely flawless, but buy the best you can.

How to care for them: Like any other period textile, tablecloths should be treated with TLC. If they're in perfect shape, I throw them into the washer with my delicates, and tumble dry on low. (If I'm washing anything with lace, it always gets hung to dry. If linens need some stain removal or color-boosting, I use my tried-and-true soaking method (see handkerchief curain). With patience, most stains are removable.

Table Linens

Table linens are located in the Dining & Bar category within Home & Garden, or you can explore the Antique and Collectible categories for unique vintage pieces. For holiday decorating, check eBay regularly for tablecloths and runners that fit the season. Shop early, or after a holiday to find great deals on Christmas and other holiday linens.

Curtains

The kitchen is the perfect place for bright, cheerful curtains like these, which were once a romantic tablecloth.

Placemats

The fun thing about these placemats was that I was able to use the tablecloth's interesting border as the bottom edge of the mats.

Here's a unique way to use a favorite woven wool blanket: as a tablecloth for a springtime brunch.

A Blanket Story

How to buy blankets and spreads: As already mentioned, you can get great deals on textiles you plan on transforming by purchasing "cutters." It's never cost-effective to buy perfect pieces if you're just going to end up cutting them up into pieces.

How to care for them: Cotton spreads and blankets can be machine washed, on a gentle cycle, and hung to dry. Wool varieties can be washed in the machine as well, but be sure the spin cycle isn't harsh. Otherwise, it's best to handwash woolens in a large tub. When storing spreads and blankets, be sure to keep them in a cool, dry place, with mothballs (or lavender and cedar sachets) to keep pesky bugs away. Never put anything into storage that hasn't been cleaned first: invisible stains can do damage if left alone. Don't fold items too tightly, to make sure your textiles don't get musty.

How to display them: If you choose to hang blankets or spreads, you'll want to sew a rod pocket onto the length of the back for hanging—this will make sure you don't stress the fibers in the fabrics.

It seems that along with everything else I collect, I've come to find myself with a large collection of blankets. I love all kinds of chenille bedspreads, colorful Beacon-style blankets, and patchwork quilts. They're a fun thing to collect because they're also practical: as my brother would say, "Everyone needs a blanket."

These are great items to buy online, because you have so many options to choose from. Whether you're seeking blankets to use creatively—or merely for sleeping under—you'll always find active auctions. Since there are so many blankets, bedspreads, and quilts out there, items like chenille bedspreads start at under $10.

If you're looking to sew things (like the pillows shown on page 82), you'll save a lot of money by searching for what sellers refer to as "cutters." Cutters are blankets, spreads, or quilts that are in some way ripped, stained, or damaged, but still have enough life in them to be "cut" and transformed into something else. (That pillow I mentioned? It came from what was half a blanket I'd bought. Yes, half. That fact made it very affordable: It cost me less than $5.)

Bedding

Attractive sheets, along with sets of shams and pillowcases, make a bedroom look sophisticated and welcoming. You can find great deals on brand new luxury bedding on eBay, including many popular brands, such as Ralph Lauren, Tommy Hilfiger, Nautica, Laura Ashley, Calvin Klein, Hotel Collection, and more. Try searching for high thread-count sheets by typing thread-count numbers, such as 400, 600, or 800. If you are shopping for a particular size bed, be sure to restrict your results to that size. You can either browse through the category structure (by product type, then by size) or use a keyword to indicate a size, such as King. Avoid using the word "size" in the search box, as not all sellers will include this word in their titles. If you are searching for a size that might be spelled multiple ways, include them all in your search using parentheses, and commas (for example, "Cal King, California King").

When seeking bed linens, be aware that European pillowcases are large squares, instead of the rectangles that we are used to. Also, a European duvet is not the same as our "duvet cover." A European duvet is a decorative sheet that fastens on top of a blanket cover.

Know, too, that vintage sheets might not fit the bed you sleep in: modern mattresses are thicker and bigger. A lot of vintage sheets are for "three-quarter" beds, which, as you might guess, are three-quarters the size of today's full-sized bed. You won't find vintage sheets in queen- or king-size, because beds that large weren't popular until our generation. So, as a word of advice, be sure to get all the measurements of bed linens before you bid.

ABOVE: Vintage tablecloths and other fabrics can be transformed into shades, chair coverings, or bed linens. Sometimes, you can also find bolts or cut lengths of vintage yardage to use for design projects.

OPPOSITE: Nothing says luxury like a sumptuously made bed, complete with a profusion of soft, fluffy pillows.

① After washing and drying lace, and repairing any loose pieces, iron with a steam iron. Keep the iron as cool as possible to get the job done; most vintage lace pieces don't come with fabric content labels!

② Center your pressed lace right side down in the middle of the frame you've chosen, making sure that it doesn't hang over the edges.

③ Place bottom of frame on top of back side of lace. Be sure the lace isn't bunched up or creased before securing back. A document frame or fabric back frame will work nicely.

Framed Lace

Lace is made in all different types of fabric and patterns. I feel it's all lovely and unique, and there is no other decorating scheme that can make a room feel more feminine.

Take the lace I chose. Patterned with a pair of thoroughbreds, it clearly was crafted to show a deep love of horses. While the lace's origin and age is unknown, the pair of horses look as though they're posing for a pre-race portrait. The image is softened by the fact that this rendering is made of fabric and embroidery.

When seeking lace to frame, look for pieces that reflect your personality. Search in the lace sections of auctions, and use keywords to find desired patterns.

How to buy lace: Antique lace is abundant, everywhere from online auctions to your grandmother's attic. Because there's so much out there, it's a buyer's market: unless you're seeking something of historic or antique value, you never have to spend a lot on your purchase.

There are many, many types of lace: Battenberg, cutwork, crochet, filet crochet, bobbin, lino—the list is endless. Research what you like by spending time on eBay browsing through the listings.

Before buying, ask some of the following questions: Does the seller know where it came from? How old is it? What condition is it in? Are there any loose threads or tears? Is it yellowed? (Most lace can be turned white as snow, see Hanky Sheer project, page 22.)

NOTE: If you're looking to trim items with the lace, know your dimensions. Many lace trims cannot be cut to size, because they fray and ravel when cut.

Dream Room Makeover

All of the major home furnishing stores have just one theme you have to work within. On eBay, the range is just enormous—it's your all-in-one destination.

Meera Natarajan

While Meera Natarajan might reside in Alabama, her new living room is a world away. A decorating enthusiast and avid eBay user since 2000, Meera gave her living room a contemporary makeover that reflects her interest in Asian design and Indian heritage. And she did it all for under $2,500.

To create her dream room, Meera made both big and small purchases. She set the stage with a new beige Pottery Barn sofa, armchair, and dark leather ottoman coffee table. Then, she incorporated bamboo window treatments, framed Japanese calligraphy, soft tea light, and silver-plated wall candle sconces.

Items Purchased on eBay by User ID: meera715

Large Pair Asian Look Freestanding 5 Tea Light Holders
$10.93

Pottery Barn Charleston Sleeper Sofa Without Slipcover
$761.01

New—Ikea—Fjarran Potpourri Contemporary Bowl
$17.95

4 Prints Oriental Asian Calligraphy Décor Art Print
$41.97

Pottery Barn Charleston Chair and a half Armchair—New
$449.99

Pottery Barn Charleston Sofa Slipcover Oat Suede 96"
$489.99

New Leather Ottoman Coffee Table Dark Brown/Espresso 40
$391.00

Used Target 9 Cube Bookcase
$69.99

Pottery Barn Silverplate Wall Candle Sconces
$27.77

Total Spent $2,425.10

CHAPTER

5

TABLETOPS

Be Our Guest

Nothing reflects your taste and personality quite like your table. The sparkle and twinkle of cut glass, the perfume of fresh flowers, the sleek design of white china set with a lively array of mismatched tumblers... a mixture of informality and beauty, luxury without extravagance, there is something for every taste, style, and occasion to be found everyday on eBay.

eBay is a great place to find vintage dishware to build or start a collection. Everything from pitchers, salt and pepper shakers, tea sets, and vases can be found in pristine condition online.

The table is where friends and family gather for conversation and togetherness, for nourishment and good times. And every table, whether dining or kitchen, offers the opportunity for using pretty and original eBay finds. With a little creativity and imagination, those old silver pitchers can become sparkling vases for floral displays, old jelly jars can substitute for delicate glassware (a good idea when serving youngsters), and an old quilt can become a lively table covering. The possibilities are endless.

When it comes to dinner and glassware, newer items can be mixed with vintage pieces for an eclectic look. Fiestaware and other pottery pieces, old-fashioned milk glass, and enameled tins are among the many collectible tabletop items that are both utilitarian and decorative. Also, many old kitchen appliances continue to function as well as charm, though there are some that are now more decorative than useful.

Popular categories for vintage manufacturers include Bauer, Fiesta (Vintage), and Hall & Watt. Popular searches and categories for china and dinnerware include: Blue Ridge, Flow Blue, Herend, Masons, Meissen, Red Wing, Stoneware, and Villeroy & Boch.

Since most of the vintage items you will find on the site are one-of-a-kind treasures, it is important that you know what you are looking for before you begin your search. Define your style and then educate your eye. This way, when the perfect piece becomes available, you will recognize it immediately and hopefully add it to your collection.

FILL IN THE BLANKS

Looking for replacement pieces for your china? eBay is the place to start. Just type in your maker and/or pattern to see what's available. If the piece you are looking for isn't up for sale at the time, you can save your search and have eBay mail you whenever new items are listed that match your search results. Here's how:

* Type in your search with the maker and pattern (for example, Wedgwood Turquoise Florentine)

* Click on the link in your search results labeled "Add to Favorites"

* You will then have the option to check a box and have eBay e-mail you whenever there are new items that match your search.

Assorted dishware attractively displayed in a glass-fronted closet or on an open shelf adds a lively splash of design and bright color to a kitchen or breakfast nook.

Glassware

Glasses are sold as singles, pairs, and sometimes even in sets of twelve or more. If you don't find a whole set you like, don't despair—mixing and matching different patterns in the same hue makes each setting its own statement. For a nice idea, accent your table with vintage wineglasses or water goblets in lovely jewel tones. Type in the color you are looking for; ruby and amethyst are especially popular, but Depression-era glass was made in nearly all the shades of the rainbow, from yellow to peach to blue to orange. You can decorate by color for the season, time of year, or even by holiday. Popular searches and categories for glassware include: Carnival glass, Depression glass, Princess House, Fire King, Pyrex, Heisey, milk glass, vintage Vaseline glass, Waterford, and Fostoria.

Round out your—or your grandmother's—crystal to set a table for sixteen! It's easy and fun to look for replacement pieces on eBay. Just search by the maker and pattern name.

ABOVE: Table runners in exquisite fabrics and candlesticks in assorted styles can transform a plain tabletop into a showpiece. For a unique idea, try making a table runner using vintage lace or crochet trim. (Photo courtesy of Jazzy Decor.)

BELOW: A bright bouquet of flowers can add fresh color and scent as a centerpiece, or place the bouquet on a windowsill to bring a bit of the outdoors indoors. Look for creative containers, like this antique tin pitcher, to show off the bouquet.

Flatware

Looking for new silver flatware? On eBay, you can find complete sets of sterling flatware, even in the original boxes, for very reasonable prices (these make great wedding gifts too!). There is also a wide selection of hollowware and silver plate in fun unique shapes to match your style, from art deco to Victorian. Collect different monogrammed flatware to make a full set that is whimsical, unique, and perfect for everyday use (Just click on Antiques and enter the search "silver monogram*"). Popular searches and categories for flatware include: sterling silver, Georg Jensen, Tiffany, Gorham Chantilly, and Christofie.

Table Linens

Don't save linen napkins for special occasions. By purchasing linens on eBay, you can afford to stock up on dozens of new or vintage napkins in all colors and styles to use year-round. Use vintage fabric cocktail napkins to add a classy touch to your next party. You can pick up a dozen for less than a dollar each. To add even more flair and to spark conversation, pick a few different sets from the more unusual themes. You can find embroidered images ranging from birds to poodles to fish and hillbillies. There is also a wide selection of tablecloths to choose from.

Dishware

Dishware is available in either full sets (even new in the box!) or piece by piece. If buying a set, be sure to check the number of place settings included. You can choose from traditional all-white patterns or try something more colorful like Fiestaware, which can be found both new and in vintage condition. eBay is also a great place for finding replacements for missing or broken pieces. Or fill out your china pattern by picking up those extra teacups or serving platters missing from the original set. When purchasing dishware, be sure to examine the eBay descriptions closely. Ask the seller about chips, cracks, and any viewable usage.

*

Vintage Suitcase Bar

There are so many fun ways to use funky, vintage suitcases. You'll find many of them in this book, in fact, since I find these items to be stylish, cool, and very easy to reimagine as novel pieces of furniture.

One of my favorite ways to adapt a vintage suitcase is turning it into a very hip retro-style cocktail bar. I love the bygone era this project evokes: martini lunches, the Rat Pack, '50s mod, the days when single men were called bachelors and career women raised a few eyebrows. It also calls to mind another juicy piece of nostalgia: the traveling salesman and his portable bar (much-needed sustenance, I suppose, in the days before hotels offered minibars in every room).

You can take this idea several steps further, using larger suitcases to hold party food as well. (Use your best judgment here; clearly, wet and messy foods aren't a good choice. But stacked sandwiches and containers of breadsticks or nuts work just fine.)

Finally, when you're done entertaining, your suitcase bar can be used to store nonperishable bar supplies such as glassware. Be sure, also, when you close up these old suitcases, to place something inside to keep it smelling fresh: bars of fragrant soap, aromatic candles, or dryer sheets are all good to use.

What to look for: Old suitcases are plentiful, and there are many types available. Ours is a simple, striped version without straps or handles. Some have leather or alligator trim and handles that evoke a more sophisticated, high-end look. Be sure the inside fabric is intact, not ripped, stained, or mildewy.

How to care for it: Most suitcases are musty inside; that's unavoidable. The best way to get rid of odors is to use a fabric freshening spray, then place the suitcase, wide open, in the sun for several afternoons. If this doesn't work, shake a lot of baking soda inside, let it sit overnight, then vacuum it out.

Turning this simple, vintage suitcase into a bar was about as easy as, well, opening it up. I lined the bottom with some aluminum foil, simply to keep spills at bay, then arranged my liquor bottles so they'd look attractive.

This suitcase has straps on the inside of the lid—perfect for holding shot glasses and extra stirrers.

Dream Room Makeover

What makes eBay even better [than other retail shopping sites]... is how you can find things from many other stores, both new and used, and get better deals most of the time.

Brenda Mosier

Brenda Mosier, an avid eBay user and mother of three, wanted to give her daughter something she had never had before: a room of her own. For too long Brenda's youngest had to share sleeping space with her parents and brothers, at times even sleeping on the living room sofa. All that changed when Mom decided to enter eBay's Dream Room Makeover Contest. Now that once drab storage room is a magical bedroom—ideal for Brenda's little princess.

To re-create the space into a fanciful fantasy room Brenda searched eBay for everything from flooring to window treatments. Opting for soft colors and fabrics, with lots of pinks and feminine touches, Brenda fulfilled her goal to create a one-a-kind room that her daughter can go to for some playtime as well as sleep. Best of all, the new room is one her daughter can grow up in and redecorate over the years as her tastes and needs change.

Selection of items Purchased on eBay by User ID: baby4you*

Laminate Kronoswiss Flooring 7mm Fix-It Beech and Padding
$298.02
Laminate Wood Floor Installation Kit
$13.09
Fantasy Castle Window Precut Mural Décor
$58.49
Psst Pink Princess Embellished Bed Canopy
$22.29
Child's Vanity Set with Mirror and Bench
$142.27
Wallpaper Border Huge Princess Castle Horse
$54.97
Child's Table and Chairs Unfinished Hardwood
$84.99

Ready-to-Paint New Handcrafted Toddler Bed and Matching Unfinished Night Stand
$217.99
Airbrush Kit and Compressor
$104.49
Caligraphy Alphabet Stencil
$13.97
Dream Hope Believe Stencil
$9.50
Disney Princess Crown/Tiara Décor Stamp
$5.00
Princess Crown Hearts, Etc. Stencil
$3.59
Dragon Laser Stencil
$5.60
Dragon Castle Fairy Rub-On Décor Transfers
$5.99
Wizard Frog Stars Rub-On

Décor Transfers
$5.99
3 PC Rose Wall Canopy Set
$26.74
Dollhouse Bookcase
$140.25
Princess Lamp
$50.25
Girl's Fairy Tale Princess Bedroom Rug
$29.95
Nutty Artist—Two Kids Fairy Princess Prints
$17.50
Nutty Artist—Princess Fairy Tale Art Print
$10.00
Wood Toy Storage Bench Chest
$66.90

* For a full list of items purchased visit:http://pages.ebay.com/dream roomcontest/finalist2.html

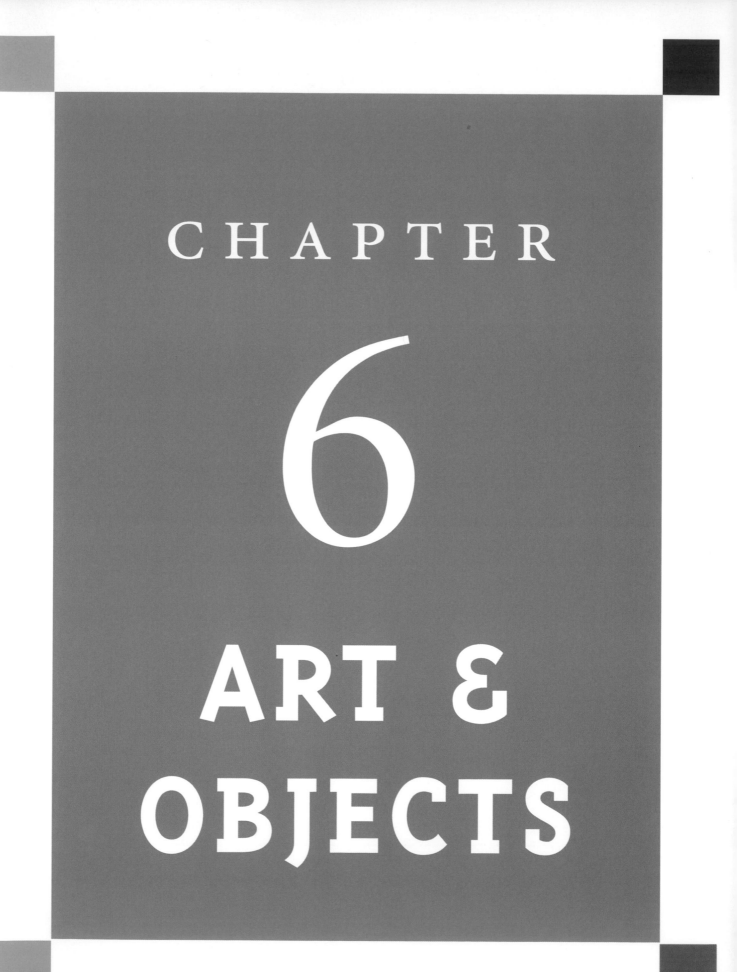

CHAPTER

6

ART & OBJECTS

Making It Personal

For me, this is where the real fun begins, the finishing touches—pulling the whole room together with the perfect paint colors, the right lighting, my collections, and the special decorative objects and accessories I've lovingly accumulated. In my home, every piece and every object tells a story; I remember where each piece of furniture came from, how each collection evolved.

When it comes to decorating, one of the best things about eBay is how often it's led me to treasures that I didn't even know I was looking for. One of my favorite unexpected discoveries involves a couple of seltzer bottles, something I have always loved but had never collected.

One day, while surfing eBay, I started searching on a lark for things using my last name, Ettinger, as the keyword. I knew there were some artists with the name but had no expectations of where else the search might lead me. I was more than delighted when my eBay Search e-mail arrived with news of a couple of beautiful seltzer bottles from the Ettinger Bottle Works, in Brooklyn, NY. Even though there's no known familial connection between me and the company, the Ettinger seltzer bottles, in a very personal way, lend a sense of history to my home. I have set up an eBay Favorite Search for my name that tells me, a few times a week, what "Ettinger" items are up for sale. My brother and I have since found a number of namesake glassware items on eBay, and we've agreed to take turns at buying.

Although I've spent years acquiring my collections and decorations, you can create individual charm and a sense of history with just a few distinctive decorative objects or accessories—a creative light fixture, one-of-a-kind artwork, a pottery collection, one magnificent vase. Don't feel you have to create the whole look overnight; add to your repertoire one beloved piece at a time.

If you find yourself with more things than you can display at any one time, just put some away for a few months, and, when you bring something back out, rest something else in its place. You can rotate things by season, display certain items when certain people are swinging by, or replace things you're tired of with those you've forgotten amid the clutter.

Decorating this way, living this way, is a process, not an end. I hope you enjoy the ride.

OPPOSITE, LEFT: Make it personal! eBay's Search function allows you to personalize your space like never before.

OPPOSITE, RIGHT: You can dress up even the simplest decorating scheme with strategically hung paintings or prints and small groupings of decorative objects. Here, a collection of brown-and-white transferware—displayed on the mantle—is set against a soft backdrop that make the objects pop.

Candles & Candleholders

Believe it or not, a candle or candleholder is sold once every minute on eBay. If you love a particular scent, you can type in the keywords for that scent to view the selection. eBay typically has hundreds of listings under vanilla, rose, and lemon. Or type "aromatherapy" to view a wide range of trendy aromatherapy candles.

Candleholders come in a varity of shapes and sizes. Look for unique candle chandeliers, candle lanterns, and elaborate candelabras along with tea light holders and hurricane candleholders. (For some clever ideas for candle displays, see Do-It-Yourself Inspiration: Luminaria Alternatives, pages 42–43.)

Fireplace Accessories

Fireplace Accessories is one of the fastest growing categories on eBay. Find beautiful, unique fireplace screens in a wide range of styles, or look for a full set of fireplace accessories. If you want to really change the look of a whole room without going to great expense, try covering grungy fireplace bricks, or any old fireplace surface that may need a lift, with a new mantel. And don't forget that mantel is a great place to display decorative objects.

Screens & Room Dividers

Screens can be used for a variety of decorating techniques—to divide a small space into separate areas, to shield a window for privacy, or to add color, style, and dimension to a corner. If you want something that will let light through, try Shoji screens made of rice paper, or screens draped with thin translucent fabrics. To add a personal touch, photo screens are a great way to display pictures of family and friends.

A Dose of Fabric

My friend Heidi had this eyesore of a screen in her basement. Before putting it to the curb, she asked if I had any ideas to bring it back to life. I went to her house, asked her for swatches of her paint colors, and left with the screen in my car. Pretty mysterious. What she didn't know, and what I suspected, was that the colors in her dining room perfectly matched this vintage fabric I'd been saving for something special. I guessed right; they were a perfect match.

Here's the story on the fabric: when I'm not buying things on eBay, I'm a seller, too. I found nearly a bolt of this '40s floral print at a yard sale, and started selling off several yards at a time online. I loved the print so much that when it came time to sell off the last of it, I decided to keep it. Not very practical, because I have more fabric than anyone I know... not to mention the fact that my entire home is decorated in shades of white. No florals, anywhere.

Redoing this screen seemed the best way to keep my gorgeous fabric nearby. I can visit it whenever I want to, yet was able to give something I love to a good friend.

How to buy fabric: Look for fabric that's been stored on a roll, or bolt, instead of folded; folds weaken the fibers. Upholstery fabric is the best kind of vintage textile to buy, because it's both heavy duty and 54" wide.

How to care for it: If it's never been washed, don't wash it yourself because colors can run or bleed. Unless the label reads "colorfast," send it to the dry cleaners to be safe. Once it's clean, protect it from stains and yellowing with a fabric protective spray such as Scotchguard™. When storing fabric, be sure it's freshly cleaned and avoid keeping it in airtight plastic storage trunks. Keep it in a cool, dry area of your home. If you're storing wool, be sure to use lavender and cedar sachets to keep moths away.

How to use it: Don't have a screen to redo? Not a problem. You can make pillows (page 82) or pillow shams, curtains, tablecloths, a shower curtain, the possibilites are endless! Just be sure you do use it; I tend to hoard fabric, and it does me no good sitting in a storage closet.

(1)

First I laid out the chosen fabric and cut each panel a few inches bigger than the screen section.

(2)

A staple-gun was then used to tack the fabric into the screen. I stapled all around the edges, pulling the fabric tight as I tacked it down. Once I was finished stapling, I cut away any excess fabric.

The Thrill of the Hunt

To most, the allure of searching for items online is the incredible variety of things you can find, often at bargain prices. Vintage pieces especially can make a home, even a new home, look lived in and loved. There are some tips you should keep in mind, though, to help you shop savvy.

First, if you are looking for the real thing, watch out for reproductions. For example, authentic vintage posters versus reproduction vintage posters: Both look excellent with a variety of decorating schemes, but you have to make sure you know what you are getting. Read the description carefully and if you are not sure, ask if it is a reproduction. Ask about the age, condition (does it have creases? is it torn or frayed?), history, etc. Ask if you can have written documentation of an item's age and provenance.

In addition to vintage pieces, there are tons of artists who sell their work through the site. Check out the "self-representing artists" category for amazing finds on original artwork in every genre and style imaginable. There are also lots of picture frames to choose from, both new and old. Antique picture frames (carved, gilt, etc.) can add a fun flare to a room and they will really change the look of a new print.

When it comes to decorative art and objects, my advice is that if you love it, you should buy it, collect it, and enjoy it. These are the treasures that make your home special.

LEFT: An antique botanical print in muted earth tones is beautifully framed by a collection of blue glass and a vintage timekeeper. Antique picture frames are very popular on eBay, and they add a unique touch to your family photos or framed artwork.

OPPOSITE: A room truly comes into its own when all of the elements—antique furniture, sophisticated wall coverings, decorative florals, and gilded framed paintings—work together in joyful unison.

Picture Frames

Because there are so many photo frames on eBay (over 5,000 at any time), it's helpful to narrow your search as much as possible before browsing through listings. Try typing specific materials, or sizes, you have in mind first. Click in the Individual Frame category to find categories for each size photo frame. Multi-photo displays and photo frame sets have become very popular. You'll find separate categories for these in the category structure on the left-hand side of the page. Also, look beyond the obvious. You may find an inexpensive work of art that is worth purchasing simply because it has a stunning frame.

To create this project you'll need a plain wooden frame, a handful of vintage dice (or other items you choose to adorn the frame with), and some clear-dry high-tack glue. Glue each die to the frame with the high-tack glue. Make sure not to move the frame at all until the glue has set.

Decorate a Frame

I never knew that I had a dice collection until I started packing my things to move to a new apartment. Am I a closet gambler? Not likely. As I sorted through years of collections, dice started showing up. Where did they come from? Who knows...a yard sale here, an estate sale there. All of a sudden I had a cache of dice.

They're made from all sorts of materials: Bakelite, ivory, and good old fashioned plastic. I'd thought for a time that I'd end up drilling them through their snake eyes and stringing them up as a necklace, but decided this is a better way to show them off.

No dice? No problem.

Frames can be decorated with an infinite number of things: vintage beads, jewelry findings, antique buttons, bingo numbers, retro sewing and embroidery notions, and miniatures. They can also be used as a background for any number of decoupage projects.

Larger frames can be adorned with old, weathered wooden clothespins—a personal favorite—playing cards, retro cutlery, and more. (Larger items must be affixed with hot glue for a sturdier hold.)

How to choose frames: Since you'll be using vintage items to decorate your frame, you don't need to use an old frame for the project unless you want a more retro look. I used a new frame, so the items—in this case, dice—pop out at you, and make more of a design statement. Choose wood or cardboard frames, so the glue will stick to them. (Painted, plastic, glass, or metal frames aren't porous, and your glued items won't stay attached for very long.)

If you'd like to distress a new, wooden frame, try using some rough sandpaper to remove the finish. You can bang it with a hammer or small metal tools—like a screwdriver—to give it an even more worn appearance. (Just make sure to remove the glass first!) If you'd like to change the color to make it seem old, you can rub some ashes onto it. Additionally, raw wood can be dyed with liquid fabric dye, which can be found at most grocery stores.

Choose frames that will complement your prints or plates. I chose a simple, unfinished wooden frame so as not to compete with the beauty of each image.

②

Mats will make your prints look like they've been professionally framed. You can choose a neutral color, as I did, or find one that picks up one of the colors in your art.

③

Carefully place the mat on the fame, then lay the print, face down, on top. Before closing the frame, look at the right side to make sure neither the print nor mat has slipped out of place.

*

Create Your Own Art

I first saw framed textbook plates—these came from an 1800s ornithology textbook—in a decorating magazine, and I immediately fell in love with the idea. Since then, I've added to my collection through eBay, and if this kind of art does it for you, auctions are a great place to start collecting.

Creating art from unusual sources is as easy as finding a vintage calendar with a botanical print theme. You'll instantly have 12 pieces of art for your walls. Nobody will know where your "artwork" comes from, and if you mat the material, it makes everything look a lot more finished and valuable.

Some other sources for instant art: pictures or ads from magazines, postcards, stationery, artbooks (I always get mine at library book sales, where they never cost more than $1 and I don't feel guilty cutting them up!), pages from children's books (for your kid's rooms), vintage sheet music (the images on the covers are fabulous) and album covers. Also look for antique family photographs and old maps. (I found a New York City subway map in a great aunt's apartment, circa 1948. After I framed mine, I saw an identical one in the window of a framing store for over $200!)

The best part about decorating with old prints is that it's fast and easy, and you can create a collection in a very short time with relatively little money.

Collecting

1. Mix traditional and contemporary pieces: When it comes to collecting, I like to combine old pieces with new ones. The older pieces add elegance and sophistication to the room and serve as a historical backdrop for contemporary ones. And the mix makes the room feel more personal and original.

2. Combine styles: Collecting in just one style can get boring. Instead, think about combining several complementary styles to create beautiful, yet fresh settings.

3. Make collections look like they've evolved over time: My best collections are the ones I added to, little by little, over time. These collections look natural and are great conversation pieces because there's a story behind every piece. So, start small (it only takes three pieces to make a collection) and look for things that mean something to you.

4. Start with your passions: When you're just starting out and don't know exactly what to collect, start with your hobbies and passions. This will give you a framework and point of reference as you begin collecting. It takes some time to learn about the marketplace, sources, prices, and what's available, so make sure you love the subject.

5. Look for the patina of age: To create an instant vintage look in any room, gather components that have an aged or well-used appearance. And not every piece needs that patina; a few well-placed items can set the overall tone of the room.

6. Accessorize in scale: Oversized furniture alters the perception of scale and makes a small room appear larger and a large room more intimate. You can achieve the same effect with your accessories. Larger, taller pieces mated with smaller-scale versions of themselves can bring high ceilings down to a more personal level.

7. Be diverse: Expand your range by collecting from a variety of places, cultures, and eras. Keep adding to them over the years so that they mature and grow with you.

LEFT: Remember the rule of three: It only takes three items to make a collection.

CENTER: If you collect by theme, such as roosters, you can find a wide variety of items—from lamps, to plates, to statuettes—to create a whimsical tabletop display.

RIGHT: Even antique sporting equipment can take on a new life when hung decoratively on a wall. Look for a variety of pieces to group together.

ABOVE: Years ago, buying original art online was an industry no-no, as you could never be sure just what you were getting. Today, with photo images, reputable dealers, and the protection of eBay pros, buying art online is gratifying and can even be profitable.

There are all sorts of unique treasures you can find on eBay to add personality to your home. Things like weather vanes, lightning rods, glass fishing floats, antique maps, antique medical equipment, and more. Many of these items are found by exploring the subcategories within Antiques: click on "Antiques" from the Home page and browse through the names of the subcategories to find something special that sparks your interest.

Mirrors are a fun way to play with spatial perceptions, and with the right frame, they can become works of art in themselves. An attractive trio, like the one pictured here, can be bought brand-new online. (Photo courtesy of Classy Yet Affordable.)

✳

Kitchenware Wreath

I don't remember where the inspiration for this wacky wreath came from. But I'm always looking for new and unique ways to show off my ever-growing collection of vintage '40s kitchenware. The collection keeps growing, it seems, because these wares are so affordable. (What you see here is only a small fraction of what I've collected!)

Eggbeaters, of which there are numerous varieties, are by far my favorite thing to collect. Prices for a pair rarely get higher than $10, if that much. Potato mashers, just like the ones your grandmother used, are also inexpensive; they sell at auction for about $2 each. Spatulas, whisks, and cooking spoons, depending on what kind of handles they bear, cost around $5. Gardening tools (like the green and red forks I have interspersed throughout the wreath) start at $1. As you can tell, a collection like this is worth it's weight in sentimental value.

Project-wise, this is a really easy one; the wreath took under an hour to create. The toughest part, really, was deciding which utensils to use, and arranging them so that they worked well together. If you're intimidated by making your own wreath base, you can always purchase one at any craft store (or online, where I've found the best prices for craft supplies).

How to buy kitchenware: Look for pieces with as little rust as possible. Look for either Bakelite handles, or wooden ones with as much paint left on as possible. Ask the seller if the piece still works (for eggbeaters, or other pieces with working parts).

How to care for it: If you decide to hang your wreath outdoors, it's imperative that you seal it with several coats of clear, rust-proof spray varnish. This will help protect it from the elements. It's also best to bring it inside for the winter.

How to display it: There are many ways to display these great old pieces of history in your home. I have a vintage egg-collecting basket in my living room, filled to the rim. I've seen other people hang the eggbeaters from their pot-racks, or turn the smaller, lighter pieces into, of all things, Christmas ornaments. You can also frame the utensils in shadow boxes, so each is its own exhibit. Retailers like The Container Store offer a myriad of products to help you showcase your collection.

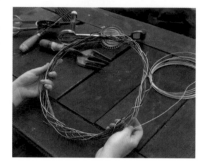

I created a base for the wreath with about five wire coat hangers. To keep these wire circles in place, I wrapped a thinner, more pliable wire all around until it became strong and sturdy.

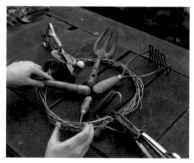

I chose the utensils I wanted to use by laying them around the wreath base and seeing which ones went best together.

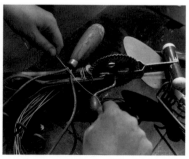

Use pliable, steel wire to attach each piece to the wreath base, wrapping it around the utensil several times until it feels secure and snug.

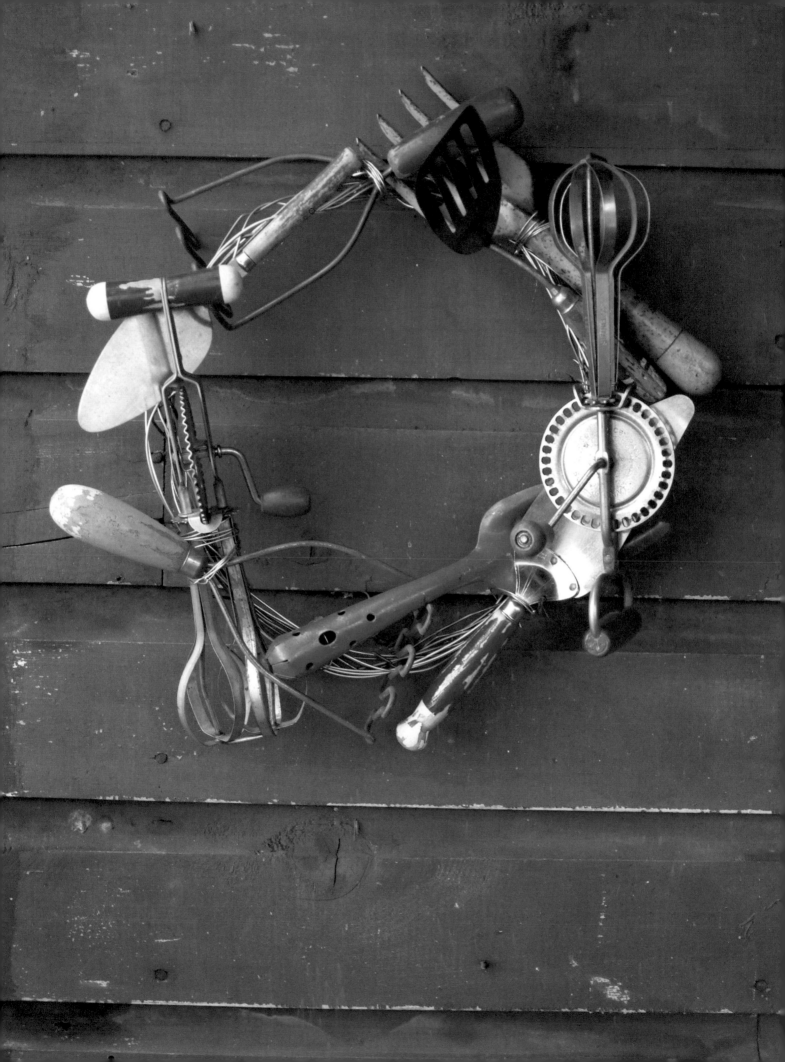

✳

Creative Containers

A plain glass florist's vase? A ho-hum terra-cotta planter? Not in my house. I don't know when I started collecting containers, but I looked around one day and my home was filled with them. As you may have already noticed, I collect kitchenware. It's easy to find, either online or at yard sales, and like everything else here, is very affordable.

When my vintage tins aren't holding plants or flowers, they are their own display. They live in my kitchen, sitting in a row, above the cabinets. They bring a retro feel to the space, and I consider them art.

I did a recent Internet search and found many new pieces for my collection, some selling for as little as $10. My ceramic coffee canister was once most likely part of a set. Old clay canister sets can be pricey, but sold solo, a canister can be very affordable—and make for a funky planter.

As for the oversized, aluminum watering can, I'll concede that it belongs to my mother. She really uses it to water her plants. I've seen a plethora of them online, in all shapes and sizes. I haven't bought my own yet for a really simple reason: I need to find a place for it first. Until then, I'll just borrow Mom's.

How to buy them: Once you start looking in earnest, interesting vintage containers are everywhere. Instead of using keywords like "pots," "vases," or "planters," search for "canisters," "cans," and "pots." Keep your costs low by purchasing well-worn items (i.e., buy ones that are old and chipped).

How to care for them: A rule of thumb for all vintage vessels: no dishwashers, ever. Handwash everything, and dry quickly to keep rust at bay. If you're using one as a vase, it doesn't have to be watertight—you can always place an unobtrusive jar inside to hold the water. If you're using one as a planter, keep it safe from rust and soil by either placing a potted plant inside, or lining the inside with foil or plastic wrap.

THIS PAGE:
Vintage ceramic kitchen canisters are creative containers for plants.

This Axelrod's Cottage Cheese can is one of the all-time favorites in my collection of metal cans.

OPPOSITE:
A rustic, old, aluminum watering can makes a wonderful country-style vase.

THE EBAY HOME MAKEOVER

Vases can be found on eBay both in the Pottery & Glass category and under Home Décor in Home & Garden. Sometimes, it's interesting to sort by price. Start with the highest, look for some unique ideas, then type in keywords to see if there is anything similar at a more appealing price point.

Hanging Bottle Vase

I have a passion for vintage glass bottles. I display small groupings of them throughout my home, look for them whenever I'm shopping either online or at yard sales, and hunt for their remains (shards of beach glass) when I'm at the ocean.

I love the way old bottles feel in my hand; they're imperfect and aren't as smooth as those made today. The glass also catches the light differently, as they're slightly opaque.

You'd probably be surprised to find that many of the bottles sold on eBay come from the dump. Years after a bag of garbage is dumped, all that's left are the milk and medicine bottles. Long before I even had an e-mail address, my brother and I stumbled on an old, country dump and spent an afternoon collecting. I later learned that other "professionals" find their wares just like I did, which is why so many bottles end up on auction sites like eBay.

What to look for: Old bottles are everywhere, and for projects like this you don't need one that's rare or valuable. You just need a nicely shaped bottle that will look good with a flower placed inside. So when you're looking through auction listings, the cheaper the better. Look for bottles with narrow necks that have lips at the end, to hold the wire securely.

How to care for them: Never put vintage bottles in the dishwasher; they could crack or shatter. The best way to clean them is in warm soapy water, using a bottle brush to remove debris from the inside.

How to display them: What a sight it would be to have an entire tree, or side of a shed, covered with hanging bottles in all different shapes, sizes, and colors! I used a steel wire to make sure the metal wouldn't rust. Another great idea would be to use copper wire, which would acquire a lovely green patina with age.

①

Wrap the wire several times around the neck of the bottle. Be sure the wire is taught right below the lip to keep the bottle from slipping out.

②

Form a loop with the wire, for hanging, and wrap the wire around itself several times to secure.

EBAY BUYER'S GUIDE

From furniture to antique rugs to down comforters . . . from draperies to fine silver to kitchen tiles . . . this "eBay Buyer's Guide" is designed to help you find fabulous, well-priced, quality items for your home, quickly and easily. I have carefully vetted every one of these sellers, setting specific criteria for inclusion, but I encourage you to evaluate your sellers carefully before you purchase.

At the time of publication (2005), every eBay seller listed in this eBay Buyer's Guide had at least a 97% customer feedback rating, based on more than 50 customer feedback submissions. That's the minimum. Most chosen sellers scored even higher.

There are thousands of popular and successful eBay sellers who have met those feedback levels—many more than we could possibly include. Use this guide, but also explore and experience eBay on your own. Make sure to comparison shop and take a look at different sellers' About Me pages and their feedback comments.

To learn how to use eBay to the max, please refer to the section "Getting Started," on page 11. You will find valuable information on how to explore the site, find great stores and merchandise, and find a specific eBay member. You will also learn about how eBay works to keep the marketplace safe. (Please note that eBay sellers and stores can change. This information was accurate at time of publication.)

Now it's time to go shopping.

Helpful Hints

Here are some other helpful tips to help you shop on eBay:

* To find a member, click on Advanced Search. On the home page it is the link located directly to the right of the search button. Then click on Find A Member and enter the sellers eBay user name.

* Other helpful info and icons:

 ME = About Me Page (sellers create this to tell you about their business)

Tag in a circle = seller has a store

by user id = feedback (click to see what % is positive)

 Power seller logo = power seller status

 = seller accepts Paypal

★ ☆ Colored star = number of feedback

⫽Buy It Now Buy it now = buy it now rather than bid at auction

* Payment Key

PP = PayPal; CC = All Major Credit Cards; V = Visa; MC = MasterCard; AMX = American Express; DIS = Discover; MO = Money Order; IMO = International Money Order; PCk = Personal Check; CCk = Cashier's Check

Windows & Walls

Photo Courtesy of D. Marie Interiors Wallpaper Décor.

Wallpaper

Billchrest (eBay User ID: billchrests)
Wallpaper borders

With over 100 borders to choose from, Billchrests is the site to visit if you want the not-so-ordinary wallpaper border. Billchrest auctions a diverse line of wallpaper borders, from toile and flower patterns, to Winne-the-Pooh and sailboats. If you're looking to enliven a child's or young adult's room, a den, or a kitchen, these borders will do the job.

Payment: PP, CC, MO, PCk, or CCk
Positive Feedback Rating: 99.7%
Selling on eBay since 2001

Home Décor and More Store (eBay User ID: decor84uandme)
Wallpaper

Home Décor auctions wallpaper with low start bids. Wallpaper patterns (either large or small) include striped, floral, and plaid, and come in a variety of colors and styles. There are Asian-inspired designs, like a bamboo and elephant print, as well as nature-inspired renderings, like the dragonfly and butterfly designs, that bring the outdoors, indoors.

Payment: PP, CC, MO, PCk, or CCk
Positive Feedback Rating: 99.1%
Selling on eBay since 2003

Webb's Wallpaper Warehouse (eBay User ID: Wallpaper10)
Discounted wall coverings and borders

Webb's Wallpaper Warehouse offers thousands of high-quality, name brand wall coverings and unique borders at 60-90% discount. All of their products are guaranteed and they agree that no purchase is complete until the buyer is satisfied. With over 700 colorful patterns that can be viewed online, there is a vast array of choices for every room in the house. If the potential buyer is looking for a pattern not listed, Wallpaper10 will try to locate it at a bargain price. An eBay Powerseller, Wallpaper10 boasts the best possible feedback score from thousands of satisfied customers.

Payment: PP, CC, MO, PCk, or CCk
Positive Feedback Rating: 100%
Selling on eBay since 2001

Photo Courtesy of Wallpaper Expo

Window Treatments

Ann's Home Décor and More
(eBay User ID: craftyannscorner)
Window treatments

Ann's Home Décor and More provides a large selection of new window treatments, including stunning discounted items from the Martha Stewart, JCPenney, and Ikea collections. Pictured items include panels, draperies, kitchen curtains, and swag sets as well as curtains designed for children's rooms. Shower curtains, candles, and bathroom accessories are also available. Ann's Home Décor and More is an eBay Powerseller.

Payment: PP, CC, MO, or CCk
Positive Feedback Rating: 99.3%
Selling on eBay since 2003

Photo Courtesy of Indian Selections.

MSJ4854 (eBay User ID: MSJ4854)
Hard-to-find window treatments

MSJ4854 provides the home decorator with a variety of unusual window treatments such as embroidered and jacquard draperies, lace and velvet draperies, and crystal sheers. The seller also carries satin pillowcases, beaded shower curtains, and embroidered or gold bathroom accessories as well as unusual bath rug sets.

Payment: PP, CC, MO, or CCk
Positive Feedback Rating: 99.7%
Selling on eBay since 2000

JuliaP30 Kid's Curtains and More (eBay User ID: Juliap30)
Window treatments for children's rooms

As the name suggests, Juliap30 sells new handcrafted curtains to delight children. Her current collection features all the kids' favorites—Nascar, Scooby-doo, Barbie, Spider-Man, Sponge-Bob Squarepants—and a variety of popular sports logos and designs. The picture gallery also features a wide variety of vivid valences in designs that appeal to grown-ups.

Payment: PP, CC, MO, or CCk
Positive Feedback Rating: 100%
Selling on eBay since 2003

Armoires and Accents (eBay User ID: pbstyle)
Draperies

Armoires and Accents recently opened a new retail store in San Antonio, Texas, and is committed to helping the consumer find quality home décor from around the world at heavily discounted prices. Their eBay store features a selection of silk dupioni curtain drapes and silk panels—in colors ranging from mushroom to ruby, copper to slate—all with free shipping.

Payment: PP, CC, MO, or PCk (PP preferred)
Positive Feedback Rating: 98.6%
Selling on eBay since 2002

Look-bambooblinds-ca
(eBay User ID: look-bambooblinds-ca)
Unusual blinds and more

Look-Bambooblinds, an eBay Powerseller, specializes in unusual, hard-to-find window treatments such as Japanese rice paper blinds, bamboo roll-ups, bamboo match stick blinds, Roman shades, and Reed Designer Blinds. Window treatments, however, are only the beginning. It also features place mats, gift baskets, even incense sticks, and an unusual variety of items for crafters, especially origami paper.

Payment: PP, CC, or MO
Positive Feedback Rating: 98.3%
Selling on eBay since 2002

Flooring & Lighting

Rugs

Sweet Lemon Bazaar (eBay User ID: sweetlemonbazaar)
Mix of new and antique rugs

Sweet Lemon Bazaar sells high-quality vintage Persian rugs. Carpets range in size from 1' x 2' to 9' x 12', and there is a variety of runners and round and oval rugs. Detailed information about each auction includes the rug's country of origin, size, foundation, pile, condition, color, age, shipping price, weave, and KPSI (knots per square inch). For oversized carpets, like an original Kashan that measures 13'8" x 9'8" see sister site, Chateau Rugs.

Payment: MO, PC, or CCk
Positive Feedback Rating: 98.9%
Selling on eBay since 2003

Top Rug (eBay User ID: toprug)
Vintage Persian rugs with diverse styles

Top Rug offers a diverse range of Persian rugs, circa the 1920s. The hand-knotted rugs include Kirman, Tabriz, Sarouk, and Isfahan. They come in a range of sizes and most have high KPSI numbers. Check out the stellar feedback comments on this site.

Payment: PP, MO, or CCk
Positive Feedback Rating: 99.5%
Selling on eBay since 2003

Natural Home Rugs (eBay User ID: sisalmills)
Rugs made from natural materials

Natural Home Rugs auctions large area rugs made from one of four earth-toned, natural materials: sisal, sea grass, mountain grass, or bamboo. These rugs are highly resistant to stains and dirt, and they are easily cleaned with a broom. Each rug comes with nonslip latex backing and 2 3/4"-wide topstitch binding, available in cream, adobe, sage, green, red, navy, black, brown, or auburn. They are available in nine sizes, from 2' x 3' to 12' x 15'.

Payment: PP, CC, MO, PC, or CCk
Positive Feedback Rating: 100%
Selling on eBay since 2004

Home Innovations (eBay User ID: home_innovations)
Contemporary area rugs

Home Innovations auctions quality, contemporary area rugs and runners. These handmade wool rugs, which measure 5' x 8', are designed in unique, contemporary styles, adding interest to any modern décor.

Payment: PP, CC, MO, PC, or CCk
Positive Feedback Rating: 99.5%
Selling on eBay since 2001

Ark Rugs (eBay User ID: ark_rugs)
Antique Persian rugs

The rugs auctioned on this site are woven in Kashmir, Afghanistan, or Iran. The ornate and beautiful pieces begin with low start bids, some as low as just $.99. This often leads to competitive bidding—just the thing that makes eBay unique in the online world.

Payment: PP, CC, MO, PC, or CCk
Positive Feedback Rating: 99.1%
Selling on eBay since 2001

Premium Carpets (eBay User ID: premiumcarpets)
New, hand-knotted Persian rugs

Premium Carpets sells beautiful, hand-knotted Persian and Chobi Oriental rugs. There are hundreds of unique carpets to choose from, each with intricately designed patterns. Sizes range from small to oversized. Premium Carpets also auctions runners, and oval and round rugs.

Payment: PP, MO, PC, or CCk
Positive Feedback Rating: 97.6%
Selling on eBay since 2001

Style Market (eBay User ID: stylemarket)
Newly handmade rugs

Style Market auctions hand-knotted rugs from Iran. There are hundreds of carpets to choose from, each with a design unique to this site. Sizes range from small to oversized, and Style Market also auctions runners, and oval and round rugs. Bidding on some rugs starts as low as $10.

Payment: PP, MO, PC, or CCk
Positive Feedback Rating: 98.4%
Selling on eBay since 2004

California Rug (eBay User ID: californiarug)
Contemporary area rugs

California Rug auctions contemporary area rugs and runners, woven with vibrant colors and bold designs. From pared-down designs to those with a lively appeal, these rugs will work in a variety of modern décors. California Rug also sells Persian-inspired rugs and runners. Bidding for the largest of these pieces begins at a modest $90.

Payment: PP, CC, MO, PC, or CCk
Positive Feedback Rating: 99.3%
Selling on eBay since 2002

Regency Rugs Super Store (eBay User ID: regencyrugs)
Ornate area rugs

Regency auctions rugs that are made of synthetic materials like polypropylene and polyolefin, which keeps prices at a mid-range start bid. Of the 500 rugs up for auction, many are Persian-styled while others are fashioned in a French Regency style.

Payment: PP, MO, or CCk
Positive Feedback Rating: 99.1%
Selling on eBay since 2001

Rugday.com (eBay User User ID: Rugday.com)
A wide variety of discounted area rugs

Rugday offers a vast variety of area rugs to please every taste, everything from an Egyptian King Tut's Sarcophagus design to traditional Aubussons and bamboos. African, Southwestern, Navajo as well as Persian and contemporary designs round out their impressive inventory. Sizes range from 5 x 8 to 8 x 11, plus runners and circular rugs.

Payment: PP, CC, MO, or PCk
Positive Feedback Rating: 99.9%
Selling on eBay since 2001

Chocolate Covered Cherries (eBay User ID: 4mililcowboys)
Pottery Barn rugs and more

Chocolate Covered Cherries, an eBay Powerseller, is the place to go for catalog returns as well as brand new items and over-stocks from Pottery Barn, Pottery Barn Teen, and Pottery Barn Kids. Its collection of area rugs features everything from hand-knotted Persians to Serape and Gabbeh rugs at unbeatable prices. Not limited to rugs, it also carries an impressive line of Pottery Barn bedding and window treatments.

Payment: PP, CC, MO, or CCk (prefers PP)
Positive Feedback Rating: 99.4%
Selling on eBay since 2000

Designer Rug (eBay User ID: Designerrug)
Deluxe Oriental rugs

Designer Rug offers magnificent, one-of-a-kind, hand-knotted Oriental rugs. Many are high-end traditional rugs of unusual quality for the discriminating buyer, but the store offers some-thing for everyone. These rugs are guaranteed genuine Orientals. Many are silk, some vegetable-dyed wool. A number are antique carpets of superb quality. The wide variety and bril-liant colors of these beautiful carpets will enhance any décor.

Payment: PP, CC, MO, or PCk
Positive Feedback Rating: 98.9%
Selling on eBay since 2001

Pakobel Rugs (eBay User ID: Pakobelrugs)
Rugs at unbeatable prices

Pakobel Rugs is a liquidator of authentic hand-knotted semi-antique and antique Oriental rugs. With a large collection for sale at any time, there's something for any decorating scheme. The rugs come in all sizes from extra large room size to tiny Kilims. An eBay Powerseller, it offers the lowest prices on its carpets as well as low shipping costs.

Payment: PP, CC, MO, PCk, or CCk
Positive Feedback Rating: 99.5%
Selling on eBay since 2002

NYC Rugs (eBay User ID: NYCrugs)
Oriental rugs

NYC Rugs operates out of a 500-square-foot showroom in midtown Manhattan and maintains an enormous inventory of antique Oriental rugs as well as newer traditional and contem-porary designs. Pictured items include Caucasian carpets, Turkoman rugs, antique Persians, Indian Agra rugs, Pakistani Sumack and Afghan Tribal Wool Kilim rugs, as well as Aubusson French-style carpets and many, many more, all at excellent prices.

Payment: PP, CC, MO, or PCk
Positive Feedback Rating: 99.8%
Selling on eBay since 2001

Manhattan Oriental Rugs
(eBay User ID: manhattanorientalrugs)

Oriental rugs in a variety of sizes

Manhattan Oriental Rugs, an eBay Powerseller, is a family-owned business that has been operating from the heart of Manhattan's rug district for over 20 years. They import from all over the world, offering the buyer a huge selection of exceptional new and antique handmade carpets, everything from Agras to Tabrizes. Rugs come in traditional and hard-to-find sizes as large as 12' x 18' and 10' x 14'. Many square rugs are available as well as standard runners and stair runners over 25' long.

Payment: PP, CC, MO, or CCk
Positive Feedback Rating: 98.9%
Selling on eBay since 1999

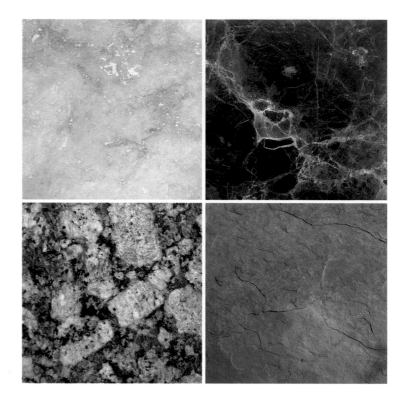

Flooring

All Ceramic Tile and Bisque (eBay User ID: weegeegirl2)

Rialto Stone and Ceramic Tile

All Ceramic Tile and Bisque specializes in tile—ceramic murals, accents, and border tiles in all sizes and designs. The store also offers Rialto stone tile, which looks like stone or tumbled marble. If the potential buyer sees a design in ceramic tile, but would prefer Rialto stone, this seller will try to find it.

Payment: PP, CC, MO, or CCk
Positive Feedback Rating: 100%
Selling on eBay since 2002

Aristophanes Murals (eBay User ID: aristophanesllc)

Tile murals

Aristophanes Murals provides unique tiles for indoor walls in virtually every room in the house, everything from classic fine art to original designs. These tile murals are ceramic or marble and come in an unbelievably large variety of subject areas—Art Nouveau, Japanese, Impressionism, to name only a few. Whether the buyer wants a nude tile mural for a bathroom, a Monet backsplash, or a Van Gogh design, this site, with over 100 pages of pictured murals, will have the item.

Payment: PP, or CC
Positive Feedback Rating: 100%
Selling on eBay since 2000

Photo Courtesy of BuildDirect.

Mexican Touch (eBay User ID: mexicantouch)
Talavera tiles

Mexican Touch sells Bellisima Talavera Tiles in solid colors and traditional designs and in a variety of lot sizes. This art style originated in Puebla, Mexico, and all products sold by Mexican Touch are handmade in Mexico with satisfaction guaranteed. The site offers the potential buyer photographs of brilliantly colored tiles in many unusual patterns.

Payment: PP, or CC (prefers PP)
Positive Feedback Rating: 100%
Selling on eBay since 2004

Tesoro de Mexico (eBay User ID: Piloto944-mx)
Vivid tiles from the heart of Mexico

The bright yellows, oranges, greens, and blues of the Mexican desert come vividly to life in this large collection of Tesoro tiles, richly displayed by Tesoro de Mexico. Themes are tied to the starry skies, day and night, to the desert cacti . . . all capturing the spirit and beauty of Mexico. Most sell in quantity for less than $1 each.

Payment: PP, CC, MO, CCk, or PCk
Positive Feedback: 99.4%
Selling on eBay since 2002

Build Direct (eBay User ID: builddirect)
Flooring

Quite new to eBay, but not new to offering discounted prices on their products, Build Direct is a global wholesaler of all kinds of building materials. It offers flooring at a small markup direct from the manufacturer. The site features porcelain, granite, and marble floor tiles in a variety of colors. Glueless laminate flooring is available as well as hardwood flooring in maple, bamboo, oak, Brazilian cherry, and other finishes. The site also sells decking and roofing materials.

Payment: PP, CC, or MO
Positive Feedback Rating: 100%
Selling on eBay since 2002

Dalton Flooring Liquidators (eBay User ID: daltonflooringliquidators)
Laminate flooring and tile

Dalton Flooring is a complete flooring center that has been in business for over 50 years and is dedicated to beating the prices of nationally advertised retail stores. They sell porcelain and travertine tiles, as well as Durastone slate limestone tile in a variety of colors and designs. In addition, tongue-and-groove wood flooring is available in oak, bamboo, and other finishes. The site also sells equipment such as tile cutters and Do-It-Yourself videos and DVDs.

Payment: PP, CC, MO, PCk, or CCk
Positive Feedback Rating: 97%
Selling on eBay since 2001

Photo Courtesy of Hardwood Brokers.

Lighting

The Chandelier Store (eBay ID: lightingforyou)
Unique brass and glass chandeliers and lamps

The Chandelier Store sells a variety of chandeliers and lamps. Chandeliers include a unique brass chandelier with U-drop crystals. Their brass chandeliers are a good choice, because you can either clean and polish them to keep them shiny, or, let the metal patina with age, giving them a time-worn appeal. There are also chandeliers and lamps with glass flower shades and chandeliers in petite sizes.

Payment: PP, CC, MO, PC, or CCk
Positive Feedback Rating: 99.4%
Selling on eBay since 1999

Great Chandeliers (eBay ID: greatchandeliers)
Classically-designed bronze and cast iron chandeliers

Whether placed in an entryway or foyer, these magnificent chandeliers make a bold statement. True to the Empire originals, these chandeliers are cast in solid brass and cast iron and are fashioned in a manner that has been handed down from European artisans for generations. Dressed in 24% lead hand-cut crystals, these chandeliers are characteristic of those that decorated the finest chateaus and palaces of Europe. They reflect a time of class and elegance that is sure to lend a special atmosphere to any home.

Payment: PP, CC, MO, PC, or CCk
Positive Feedback Rating: 99.1%
Selling on eBay since 1998

Photo Courtesy of Lamps Plus.

Photo Courtesy of Lamps Plus.

Lights64 (eBay ID: lights64)

Interior and exterior light fixtures

Lights64 is a family-owned business based in Chicago and founded in 1912. The business has successfully launched their eBay store and sells much of their wares online. They have hundreds of fixtures, from beautiful chandeliers and ceiling fixtures to outdoor lighting solutions. You'll also find hard-to-find bulbs, or you can contact Lights64 for assistance with finding bulbs for not-so-ordinary fixtures.

Payment: CC, MO, PC, or CCk
Positive Feedback Rating: 99.8%
Selling on eBay since 2002

Steve's Sea Gull Bargain Basement (eBay ID: steveatseagulllighting)

All types of classic lighting fixtures

New Jersey-based Steve's Sea Gull auctions lighting fixtures for any décor. If you're looking for classic lighting solutions for a good price, like a foyer fixture, you'll find it here. Most auctions start in the $20 range. Steve's also auctions outdoor lighting solutions, like an outdoor pole lantern with a solid brass finish. Descriptions include the housing base and the maximum voltage for the piece.

Payment: PP, CC, MO, PC, or CCk
Positive Feedback Rating: 100%
Selling on eBay since 2001

Photo Courtesy of Lamps Plus.

Lighting and Kitchen Closeouts (eBay ID: sjl_imports)

Ornate multi-tier chandeliers

This store is great if you're looking for ornate yet modern chandeliers for larger spaces. With modern designs, including lampshades, and width sizes over 3', these are great for large areas that need a touch of elegance. You'll find some great brands, including Swarovski and Milano. If you're looking for more classic chandeliers, they also carry traditional, crystal-style pieces.

Payment: PP, CC, MO, PC, or CCk
Positive Feedback Rating 99.2%
Selling on eBay since 1999

Photo Courtesy of Lamps Plus.

Lamps Plus Clearance (eBay ID: lampsplusclearance)
Chandeliers, bathroom and hallway fixtures, and outdoor lighting solutions

Lamps Plus offers over 500 light fixtures for auction. The classic chandeliers have competitive start bids. Chandeliers include a 21-light, 3-tier, cast bronze piece that measures 53 1/2" x 56" (complete with a 6' chain). The site great sconces, pendant lights, and bar lights for hallways, entranceways, and bathrooms. Outdoor lighting solutions include an extensive array of wall lanterns, in bronze and brass.

Payment: PP, CC, MO, PC, or CCk
Positive Feedback Rating: 98.7%
Selling on eBay since 2002

Wholesale Authority (eBay ID: wholesaleauthority)
Chandeliers and hanging light fixtures

Wholesale Authority carries light fixtures with low start bids. Great for tall entranceways or formal dining areas, the hanging pieces auctioned on this site will add a subtle accent to any décor. They are designed and manufactured by Kichler Lighting, a four-time winner of the Arts Award, a high accolade in the lighting industry. Beautiful, functional, and competitively priced, these pieces are great decorative lighting solutions.

Payment: PP, CC, MO, PC, or CCk
Positive Feedback Rating: 99.7%
Selling on eBay since 2002

Tiffany Direct (eBay User ID: michelle-nj)
Tiffany lamps

Tiffany Direct shares the dream of Louis Comfort Tiffany to put Tiffany lamps in every house. Their art lamps are crafted using Tiffany techniques and range in style from classic to modern. The site offers a wide selection of table lamps, but also window panels, wall sconces and chandeliers, literally something for every Tiffany lover and at affordable non-Tiffany, prices.

Payment: PP, CC, MO, or CCk (PP preferred)
Positive Feedback Rating: 99%
Selling on eBay since 2003

Antler Lights by CDN Antler Designs (eBay User ID: anterlights)
Rustic lighting

Because they operate from the Canadian far North with its abundance of moose, elk, white-tail and mule deer antlers, Antler Lights by CDN Antler Designs has a direct supply of natural materials and can offer high quality lighting at the best price in North America. An eBay Powerseller, Antler Lights' site offers a selection of real and reproduction antler chandeliers in a wide price range.

Payment: CC (V, MC, AE), MO, PCk, or CCk
Positive Feedback Rating: 99%
Selling on eBay since 1999

Photo Courtesy of Lamps Plus.

Photo Courtesy of EB Peters.

Living Room Furniture

EBPeters Modern Furniture (eBay User ID: ebpeters)
Modern and contemporary leather furnishings
EBPeters Modern Furniture began when the founders were unable to find quality modern and contemporary furniture on the Internet that rivaled prices at local retailers. In 2000, the company opened its eBay store to do just that, and it hopes to become the largest retailer of modern furniture on the Web. With over 16 colors to choose from, these made-to-order sofas are sure to blend with any décor. EBPeters also offers modern and contemporary barstools, dining room sets, and bedroom furniture.

Payment: PP, CC, MO, or CCk
Positive Feedback Rating: 100%
Selling on eBay since 2000

Photo Courtesy of Rialto Italia.

Out West Wholesale (eBay User ID: outwestwholesale)
Carved wooden tables to accent any living space
This wholesaler sells beautiful wooden furniture with rich appeal. Products include hope chests made from oak cedar or cherry cedar and benches made from cherry wood. With space for storage and seating, these detailed pieces are both beautiful and highly functional. Additionally, Out West sells Queen Anne–style sofa tables, coffee tables, and end tables. The curved forms of these unique pieces will add a great finishing touch to any space.

Payment: PP, CC, MO, PCk, or CCk
Positive Feedback Rating: 99.2%
Selling on eBay since 2000

SavingsHut (eBay User ID: savingshut)
Contemporary sofas and sectionals
SavingsHut offers sofa sets in sleek, modern styles with custom manufacturing on all furniture. There are three choices for upholstery—ranging from double weave cloth to microfiber to Italian leather. There are literally dozens of colors. E-mail the company to request color swatches before placing your bid.

Payment: PP, CC, MO, or CCk
Positive Feedback Rating: 98.5%
Selling on eBay since 2003

Photo Courtesy of EB Peters.

Bedroom Furniture

Old World Merchants (eBay User ID: oldworldmerchants)
Handcrafted, old-world style furnishings

Old World Merchants began by selling antique furniture from England and France in 2001. Today, in addition to European antiques, Old World sells reproduction pieces, including hand-carved furniture from Indonesia, handcrafted goods from Thailand and Turkey, replicas of Japanese antiques from Korea, and a wide range of Victorian-era replicas from China. The pieces are made of fine woods, like mahogany and elmwood, and feature unique touches, like hand-carved details, hand-fitted joints, and hand-applied lacquer finishes. An antique look is achieved through deliberately uneven application of the finish and polished brass hardware. But be sure to also check out their wonderful antiques.

Payment: PP, CC, MO, PC, or CCk
Positive Feedback Rating: 98.9%
Selling on eBay since 2001

CinJin Merchant Traders (eBay User ID: cinjin_com)
Fine Asian reproduction furniture

The retail store, St. John's Antiques, is located in British Columbia and primarily sells antiques. When Cinjin Merchant Traders opened its doors in November 2001, as St. John's online sister store, it quickly grew into a store that also included reproduction furniture, accessories, and even marine hardware and accessories. This eBay store is invaluable for the wealth of information and history that accompanies each auction item. Before placing a bid, learn more about the origin of Tansu step chests, carved oak tables, chairs, and Regency style painting tables.

Payment: PP, CC (V/MC), IMO, or WT
Positive Feedback Rating: 99.3%
Selling on eBay since 2001

DFLfurniture.com Store (eBay User ID: dflfurniture)
Classic-style bedroom furniture sets

If you're looking for classic and sturdy bedroom sets, DFL Furniture is the store to visit. Some bedroom sets are constructed with pure mahogany, while others are made with different types of hardwood, like cherry wood. Furniture sets include your choice of a king- or queen-sized bed (headboard, footboard, and rails), two night stands, an armoire, a dresser, and a mirror. The ornate carvings on the surface of the wood add an elegant touch to these pieces. Details like felt-lined drawers, with dove-tailed joints, and roller bearing gliders ensure a long life and make these pieces a good investment.

Payment: PP, CC, PC, or CCk
Positive Feedback Rating: 98.4%
Selling on eBay since 2002

Photo Courtesy of AMB Furniture.

Discount Furniture Outlet (eBay User ID: Graciesmom2002)
Unique wooden furniture

Discount Furniture Outlet starts the bidding on its high-quality furniture at great prices, sometimes as low as $199. You can find many types of furniture here, from country-style cedar chests to classic cherry wood bookcases to armoires, curio cabinets and swivel bars. Great product descriptions accompany crisp photos. Many items are offered with free shipping. Discount Furniture Outlet also sells standing mirrors, desks, beds, and islands for the kitchen.

Payment: PP, MO, PCk, or CCk
Positive Feedback Rating: 99.7%
Selling on eBay since 2002

Elegant Furnishings (eBay User ID: elegantfurnishings)
Bedroom sets for large rooms

Just read some of the great comments left for Elegant Furnishings, and you'll see why they've earned such a high feedback rating. They ship quickly, are easy to communicate with, and deliver quality pieces. Names like "Grand Mansion Suite" describe their bedroom furniture well—you'll need plenty of space for these king-sized sets. Made with hardwoods, you can add on to the set by purchasing the matching armoire, mirror, or additional set of drawers.

Payment: PP, CC, MO, or CCk
Positive Feedback Rating: 99.4%
Selling on eBay since 2002

Max Furniture (eBay User ID: maxfurniture)
Highly detailed bedroom sets

While these bedroom sets start at a slightly higher bidding price than most other eBay bedroom sets, take a look at the product photos. With great attention to detail, like custom hardware, recessed lighting in the headboard and dresser, etched mirrors, and ornately carved wood, these high-quality, detailed pieces are worth the extra money. Max Furniture also sells furniture for the living room, office, dining room, and garden areas.

Payment: PP, CC, PC, or CCk
Positive Feedback Rating: 98.9%
Selling on eBay since 2000

eBay User ID: decorfurn2001
Neo-classical and contemporary bedroom sets

Bidding for these complete bedroom sets begins at anywhere from $500–$2,000. With modest start bids, and a wide range of styles—from Shaker to neo-classical to contemporary—this site is worth checking out. There are also complete children's sets, which offer plenty of storage, for auction. And check out their great dining room sets.

Payment: PP, CC, MO, or CCk
Positive Feedback Rating: 98.4%
Selling on eBay since 2001

Photo Courtesy of AMB Furniture.

GiGaFurniture.com (eBay User ID: gigafurniture)
Solid pine bedroom furniture

Giga Furniture imports solid pine pieces directly from their Brazilian warehouse. Most pieces are constructed in a simple Shaker style. Bedroom sets include a king-sized bed, night stand, five-drawer chest, and TV armoire. Choose the finish you'd like, from a light honey to a rich mahogany. Giga also auctions occasional tables, stands, bookcases, glider rockers, office chairs, computer desks, curio cabinets, recliners, entertainment centers, and dining sets.

Payment: PP, CC, PC, MO, or CCk
Positive Feedback Rating: 98.7%
Selling on eBay since 1999

Raymour and Flanigan Clearance Center
(eBay User ID: raymour-flanigan_clearance_center)
Contemporary bedroom furnishings

One of the leading home furnishings retailers in the Northeast, Raymour and Flanigan opened its doors in 1947 in downtown Syracuse. Today the successful, family-owned and operated business auctions its wares on eBay, including four poster beds, mirrors, and five-drawer chests. The company ships goods to New York, New Jersey, Massachusetts, Pennsylvania, and Connecticut. Contact before bidding to make sure you are in their delivery zones.

Payment: PP, CC, PC, MO, or CCk
Positive Feedback Rating: 98.8%
Selling on eBay since 1997

Photo Courtesy of AMB Furniture.

GreatPricedFurniture.com Store
(eBay User ID: greatpricefurniture)
Beds, classic children's furniture

Great Priced Furniture, based in North Carolina, is a Web-based company that offers quality furniture from the best manufacturers in the industry. Top sellers include American Drew, Kathy Ireland By Standard Furniture, Hooker Furniture, and Pulaski. If you're looking for beautiful children's furniture, you'll find Jessica McClintock student desk and chair and beautiful cherry bedroom sets. In addition to full bedroom sets, this eBay store sells individual daybeds, canopy beds, and wooden and metal bed frames.

Payment: PP, CC, PC, MO, or CCk
Positive Feedback Rating: 99.7%
Selling on eBay since 2000

Miss Lynette's Antique Furniture (eBay User ID: misslynette)
Antique dining room and bedroom furniture

Miss Lynette's Antique Furniture sells a wide variety of classic furniture from around the world, with an emphasis on French, Italian, English, and Swedish imports as well as authentic American items. New items are listed each Thursday night. The emphasis is on unique and rare furniture pieces for the discriminating buyer, but other items for home decorating can also be found.

Payment: PP, CC, MO, PCK, or CCk
Positive Feedback Rating: 99.9%
Selling on eBay since 2001

Tricks of The Trade (eBay User ID: tricks-of-the-trade)
Antique furniture

Tricks of The Trade offers hard-to-find pieces, many bought from estate sales in the New York City, Philadelphia and Baltimore areas. They are committed to offering these pieces at auction, allowing the marketplace to dictate the price. While they specialize in furniture, most but not all of American origin, they also sell decorative items. Tricks of The Trade is an eBay Powerseller with a perfect Feedback Rating.

Payment: PP, MO, or PCk
Positive Feedback Rating: 100%
Selling on eBay since 2000

North Winds Antique Store (eBay User ID: norwinda)
Antique furniture

North Winds Antique Store specializes in unusual and authentic antique pieces. The site is limited to a few very special items such as a pine pirate's chest, a Gothic oak cabinet with carved dragons, a leaded glass Wernicke bookcase. Many pieces are Early American or Art Deco. Each piece is accompanied by several excellent and detailed photographs, showing the item from a variety of angles, inside and outside.

Payment: PP, or CC (PP is preferred)
Positive Feedback Rating: 99.3%
Selling on eBay since 1998

Dining Room Furniture

Darling Woodcraft (eBay User ID: darling_woodcraft)
Solid oak and cherry wood Shaker-style dining room sets
Darling Woodcraft has earned a reputation on eBay for great service and quality furniture. Each of their solid oak dining sets are handmade, one at a time, by Amish craftsmen in Holmes County, Ohio. These Shaker-style pieces are carefully fashioned from the highest quality oak and cherry wood on the market. A three-step varnishing, sanding, and finishing process creates a durable coating that ensures maximum heat and moisture resistance. There are 16 finishes to choose from and a custom staining option for just $80. Darling Woodcraft also sells furniture for the bedroom, garden, and living room.

Payment: PP, CC, MO, PC, or CCk
Positive Feedback Rating: 100%
Selling on eBay since 2002

The Collectors Closet (eBay User ID: thecollectorscloset)
Dining room and dinette sets
The Collectors Closet dining sets come in a wide range of materials, including antiqued white wood, glass, oak, nickel, and cherry wood. This eBay store offers a wide range of styles, from French country to modern to bistro. Matching hutches are available with most sets. In addition to the large and formal dining room furniture, you can also find dinettes for smaller dining areas. This vendor also sells furniture for the bedroom (and children's bedrooms), the office, and the living room.

Payment: PP, CC, MO, or CCk
Positive Feedback Rating: 99.7%
Selling on eBay since 1998

SAL4LESS (eBay User ID: sal4less)
Dining sets with low start bids
Sal4Less starts the bidding of some 7-piece dining sets as low as $575, making it one of the best eBay sites for great, inexpensive dining room furniture. Most sets are constructed with solid oak and ornate carved details, but there are plenty of contemporary designs made with cherry wood. The most unique set on this site is a white, antiqued wood set with curved legs and a beveled glass tabletop. Sal4Less has many dining set options, low auction prices, and the highest customer satisfaction rating.

Payment: PP, MO, or CCk
Positive Feedback Rating: 100%
Selling on eBay since 2003

MBW Furniture (eBay User ID: mbwfurniture)
One-of-a-kind dining room furnishings

MBW sells rich, mahogany dining room furniture. Many of its pieces are designed in the Chippendale style, including tables, chairs, hutches, and buffets. Table lengths vary from a 50" round table with pedal base to a 10' rectangular table. This site auctions full sets of dining room furniture as well as individual pieces. Buy a sideboard, chairs by the pair, or bid on a whole set. Some assembly is required on some pieces.

Payment: PP, CC, MO, PC, or CCk
Positive Feedback Rating: 99.6%
Selling on eBay since 1999

Rinner's and Brandon Furniture (eBay User ID: rrinner)
Antique furniture and accessories

Rinners and Brandon Furniture is based in Tulsa, Oklahoma, but the owner travels the world constantly to find the finest antiques for his store. Rinners specializes in estate furniture such as Baker, Henredon, Ethan Allen, Drexel, and Heywood Wakefield. The site pictures a variety of one-of-a-kind pieces of furniture, but clocks and jewelry are also available, especially fine antique rings for women.

Payment: PP, CC, MO, or PCk
Positive Feedback Rating: 98.6%
Selling on eBay since 1998

From Global to You (eBay User ID: fromglobaltoyou)
Antique furniture

From Global to You is a family business based in Provo, Utah. With staff in Europe and Asia, they have access to estate sales in country homes, chateaux, even castles. As a result, they sell rare finds, whether they be Eastlake, Art Deco, Chippendale, Baroque, or French Country. Antique dining room furniture is a specialty, but the site is not limited to those pieces. In addition to furniture, decorative items are also available such as candle holders, pipe stands, mirrors, and clocks.

Payment: PP, CC, MO, PCk, or CCk (PP preferred)
Positive Feedback Rating: 99.1%
Selling on eBay since 1999

Packrat Antiques Inc. (eBay User ID: packratantiquesinc)
Antique furniture and reproductions

Packrat Antiques, an eBay Powerseller, is located in High Point, North Carolina, and handles antique and reproduction furniture such as dining room sets, settees, china cabinets, curio cases, desks, accent chairs, and woven furniture. Its site also features lamps and a wide variety of "sure to please" antique decorative accessories, especially bronze and porcelain pieces. Antique garden statuary is also available.

Payment: PP, CC, MO, PCk, or CCk
Positive Feedback Rating: 98.5%
Selling on eBay since 1998

Michael J. Keene Antiques (eBay User ID: mk001)
Antiques

From a bulging 40,000 square foot warehouse near Boston, Michael J. Keene Antiques sells just about everything antique from furniture to collectibles to lighting. The eBay store features a collection of antique silver, primarily Sheffield, as well as unusual pieces of furniture, all well-pictured to give the potential bidder a maximum of information.

Payment: PP, CC, MO, PCk, or CCk
Positive Feedback Rating: 98.5%
Selling on eBay since 1998

From Europe to You (eBay User ID: fromeuropetoyou)
Antique furniture and decorative items

From Europe to You maintains warehouses in Belgium and Italy, ships by container to their Saugerties, New York, location and offers unbeatable prices. They sell a wide variety of antique European dining room and bedroom furniture, especially French pieces. Their site also offers art glass, unique decorative items for the outdoors, especially antique fountains and gazebos, marble statuary and magnificent, full-size bronze pieces.

Payment: PP, CC, MO, or PCk
Positive Feedback Rating: 98.7%
Selling on eBay since 1997

Photo Courtesy of Antique Traders

Antique Cabinet Hardware

Historical Restorations
(eBay User ID: historical_restorations)
Antique hardware
Historical Restorations is an eBay store dedicated to those attempting to authentically restore older homes. They offer hard-to-find lighting and hardware such as sconces and ceiling fixtures, bathroom towel racks, robe hooks, and door knobs to mention just a small portion of their stock. All are genuine and filled with the charm of an earlier time. Historical Restorations is an eBay Powerseller.

Payment: MO, PCk, or CCk
Positive Feedback Rating: 99.9%
Selling on eBay since 2003

MS English Imports (eBay User ID: msenglishimports)
Stained glass
MS English Imports is a premier dealer in antique stained glass with exceptional quality and a large quantity of glass. They regularly purchase stained glass from England for their Houston, Texas, warehouse and eBay store. Their site offers numerous antique windows, many in English floral design, especially the stylized English tulip. They also specialize in antique buffets and sideboards. These range from English Jacobean and Victorian to Flemish pieces in woods such as solid oak and mahogany.

Payment: PP, or CC
Positive Feedback Rating: 99.8%
Selling on eBay since 1999

Ketchyfraze (eBay User ID: ketchyfraze)
Antique hardware and tiles
Ketchyfraze specializes in Eastlake antique hardware such as doorknobs, cast iron and brass hinges, and pantry pulls. The site features giant doorknob hardware, window latch hardware, lock plates-all authentic, many items extremely rare. They also sell a collection of Nineteenth-Century Eastlake-era Mallard tiles, the work of T and R Boote of England.

Payment: PP, CC, MO, or CCk
Positive Feedback Rating: 99.4%
Selling on eBay since 2003

Sarah and Keith (eBay User ID: sarahandkeith)
Antique hardware
Located in Oregon, Sarah and Keith, an eBay Powerseller, specializes in hard-to-find antique hardware for those doing detailed and authentic home restoration. Among the items on their site are vintage screen doorknobs, wrought iron latches, Victorian and Eastlake bin pulls, shutter hinges, ornate glass and brass doorknobs, and much more.

Payment: PP, CC, MO, PCk, or CCk
Positive Feedback Rating: 99.9%
Selling on eBay since 2002

Photo Courtesy of Antique Traders

Textiles

Photo Courtesy of Indian Selections.

Jazzy Décor (eBay User ID: jazzydecor)

Asian-inspired pillow covers

Jazzy Décor, based in Ottawa, Canada, sells pillow covers straight from China. The pillows covers are designed using ancient Chinese patterns and Chinese calligraphy, on a satin brocade material. Available in rich colors like deep reds, silky blues, and golds, you can use this resource to decorate your home with an Eastern flair.

Payment: PP, MO, PC, or CCk
Positive Feedback Rating: 100%
Selling on eBay since 2002

Esthers Vintage Fabrics (eBay User ID: esthers_vintage_fabric)

Vintage fabrics

Esthers Vintage Fabrics auctions great vintage pieces. The ages of these one-of-a-kind pieces vary, but you're guaranteed to find a wonderful selection of vintage seventies material. For example, we found mod, green tulip patterns, plaids, paisleys, zebras, and floral prints on this site, and even pieces with classic comic book heroes like Wonder Woman and Superman. Fabrics include velvet, wool, and taffeta. Esthers also auctions vintage fabric trim, tassels, lace trims, and curtain tie-backs.

Payment: PP, MO, PC, or CCk
Positive Feedback Rating: 100%
Selling on eBay since 2004

MS Asian Imports (eBay User ID: msasianimports)

Fine silk fabrics

MS Asian Imports is a subsidiary of MS Imports, LLC, which began selling its wares on eBay through MS English Imports, MS Asian's sister store. The 100% pure fabrics on auction arrive from Nepal via India and Kashmir. Their line includes beaded silk dupioni from India (available in maroon, light pink, and a deep pink), embroidered silk dupioni from India (in silver, olive, bronze, and lavender), embroidered or quilted silk taffeta, and an array of cashmere. Their 5,000-square-feet warehouse is located in Houston, Texas, in the Historic Heights. The company now runs two successful stores on eBay, MS English Imports and MS Asian Imports.

Payment: PP, CC, MO, PC, or CCk
Positive Feedback Rating: 100%
Selling on eBay since 2002

Fabriccat (eBay User ID: fabriccat)
Upholstery fabrics

If you're looking for upholstery fabric, Fabriccat is a great site. They carry jacquards, stripes, flower designs, and plaid patterns. Whether you need large prints for a large room, or small prints to match a smaller space, Fabriccat will likely have what you need. Check this site often, and you'll find an occasional Shumacher toile or Waverly/Shumacher prints. Auctions for the fabrics tend to range between 2 and 9 yards, with some bids starting as low as $5.

Payment: PP, CC, MO, PC, or CCk
Positive Feedback Rating: 99.7%
Selling on eBay since 2002

Exclusive Silks (eBay User ID: exclusive_silks)
Silks textiles

Exclusive Silks imports fine silks straight from Bombay. These silks are great for covering accessories, like pillows, but would be equally at home as drapes or room dividers. With rich colors like deep purple, fuchsia, and cream, they can add a dash of color and bring a level of sophistication to your design. A real knockout is the plaid silk taffeta, in cream and blue—try it in the office for a bit of surprise glamour.

Payment: PP
Positive Feedback Rating: 99.6%
Selling on eBay since 1999

Shabby Fabrics and Hand Made Items
(eBay ID: ktdancer30)
Floral fabrics

Shabby Fabrics specializes in floral fabric patterns. With an emphasis on Laura Ashley–designed pieces, most fabrics celebrate the feminine. Some have a subtle stripe running behind the floral print, but almost all are a shade of pink. Most fabric measures less than a yard, so you'll need to bid on several pieces for a larger project.

Payment: PP, CC, MO, PC, or CCk
Positive Feedback Rating: 100%
Selling on eBay since 2001

Satin and Lace Place (eBay User ID: satinandlaceplace)
Silk, satin, and wool textiles

Ms. Ronni of the Satin and Lace Place was trained in New York City's Garment Center as a buyer and retailer, and has over 30 years of experience in the textile industry. With a sharp eye for value and quality, she brings her knowledge to bear on eBay. Take advantage of the reasonably priced silk in rich chocolate browns, ivory, and aqua. Additionally, Satin and Lace has a high yearly sales rate and fantastic customer satisfaction.

Payment: PP, MO, PC, or CCk
Positive Feedback Rating: 99.9%
Selling on eBay since 1998

David's Upholstery (eBay User ID: tackhammer52)
Upholstery and drapery textiles

David began his own business, after being raised in the decorating business via his family's home furnishings business. He and his wife Lynn have taken advantage of the eBay opportunity to expand the business, offering customers quality upholstery and drapery fabrics. When David was elected mayor of their hometown port city of Superior, Wisconsin, in 2003, Lynn took over the eBay business. As you can see by the great feedback, she's maintained the quality tradition. They carry medium- to heavyweight textiles, including cotton, tapestry and jacquards—they even have a line appropriate for use on outdoor furniture.

Payment: PP, CC, MO, PC, or CCk
Positive Feedback Rating: 100%
Selling on eBay since 2000

(eBay ID: shalimar88)
Fine textiles

Shalimar sells beautiful fabrics from top textile design houses. What makes this site exciting is the abundance of quality fabrics. For example, you might find a Schumacher upholstery fabric in green, with mauve, red, and butter stripes, a Brunschwig & Fils floral cotton print or an Old World Weavers embroidery fabric. You won't know what's on the auction block on any given day, but the search will be worthwhile.

Payment: PP, MO, PC, or CCk
Positive Feedback Rating: 99.8%
Selling on eBay since 2002

Georgia Gardens Fabric Designs (eBay User ID: fabric-lady1)

Decorative throw pillows

Georgia-based Georgia Gardens auctions decorative throw pillows from Zhao Designs. Zhao is a well-established decorators' workroom that produces draperies, table linens, bed linens, decorative pillows, and other custom-designed textile products. The pillows are fashioned from all types of textiles and colors range from bold, like gold and fuchsia, to more subdued hues, like cream and green. They are made with hidden zippers, so you can change your pillows by season at your whimsy.

Payment: PP, CC, MO, PC, or CCk
Positive Feedback Rating: 100%
Selling on eBay since 2004

(eBay User ID: nypad)

Mid-century styled pillows and drapes

NY Pad specializes in mid-century, modern styled pillows and drapes—the company was born out of a love for this style of design. Some items are constructed of rare vintage fabrics ranging from the 1940s to 1970s (all in perfect condition). Others are fashioned from fine reproduction fabrics from designers like Ray and Charles Eames, Alexander Girard, Verner Panton, and Nelson. Visit this site if you take pleasure in finishing it off the design of your home with flair.

Payment: PP, MO, or CCk
Positive Feedback Rating: 99.5%
Selling on eBay since 2000

Muimui4Shop (eBay User ID: muimui4shop)

Chinese silk brocade throw covers

This eBay site sells pillow covers with Chinese calligraphy and symbols. Words like "fortune," "wealth," and "longevity" are inscribed on the fabric. They are available in a variety of colors, including red, blue, gold, black, green, and orange. Bidding starts at just $1 for most items. Shipping is standard.

Payment: PP
Positive Feedback Rating: 100%
Selling on eBay since 2004

Indian Selections (eBay User ID: indianselection)

Window Treatments and decorative pillows from India

Indian Selections auctions wonderful sari window treatments and pillows. Vibrant colors, which are the hallmark of Indian clothes and décor, are available on this site. Fuchsia, royal blue, green, and chocolate brown make up just some of the colors of the window treatments and pillows from Indian Selections. Gold adds a layer of sophistication as a border or accent on most pieces.

Payment: PP, CC, MO, PC, or CCk
Positive Feedback Rating: 100%
Selling on eBay since 2001

Razmutt (eBay User ID: razmutt)

Vintage fabrics

Razmutt auctions vintage pieces, mostly rare and classic William Morris prints. We found gems such as an original piece from the Rose & Hubble line called "Seaweed," with soft rose-pink classical scrollwork on an ivory background, and, a long-out-of-print fabric by Woodrow Studio London, the design of which was taken from the "Leicester" wallpaper designed in 1911 by John Henry Dearle. This cotton piece has deep greens, gold, beige, rose pink, and blue. This site will remind you that good classic design will never go out of style.

Payment: PP, CC, MO, PC, or CCk
Positive Feedback Rating: 99.8%
Selling on eBay since 1999

Kyoto Collection (eBay User ID: kyotocollection)

Japanese cotton textiles

Kyoto Collection auctions yukata fabric, which has traditionally been used for making the kimono. The versatility of this fabric allows you to incorporate these pieces into various parts of your home design from curtains to pillow covers to bed spreads. And at $4 per yard, they're a great deal. The designs of these cotton textiles are playful yet refined, and would add depth to any home décor.

Payment: PP, CC, MO, PC, or CCk
Positive Feedback Rating: 99.9%
Selling on eBay since 2000

Close Out Linen (eBay User ID: closeoutlinen)
Bed linens

Close Out Linen offers bed linens from stores such as Macy's and Bloomingdales and also direct from manufacturers at excellent discounts. The site includes comforter sets and bed-in-a-bag sets as well as individual items by designers such as Ralph Lauren, Jessica Sanders, Calvin Klein, and Lillian Anderson. Most are pictured and range from twin to king size. Close Out Linens is an eBay Powerseller.

Payment: PP, MO, PCk, or CCk (PP preferred)
Positive Feedback Rating: 99.5%
Selling on eBay since 2001

Soft and Fluffy (eBay User ID: softandfluffy)
Down-filled comforters

Soft and Fluffy, as the name implies, sells natural down-filled comforters and pillows, as well as feather beds, and takes pride in being California's leading seller of quality custom-made bedding. Many items are as much as 80% below retail price. Their comforters and pillows are assembled to last, using only the best materials, and they come in a variety of sizes. Some covers are silk/cotton blends while others are all silk.

Payment: PP, CC, MO, or CCk (PP preferred)
Positive Feedback Rating: 99.3%
Selling on eBay since 1998

Egypt Collections 'Bed Linens from the Nile' (eBay User ID: egyptcollections)
High-end cotton bedding

Egypt Collections 'Bed linens from the Nile' is based in both the United States and Egypt. They supply custom-made bed sheets, pillowcases, and duvet covers, as well as regular sizes of pure, 100% Egyptian cotton sheets with high thread counts ranging from 600 to 1000. Egypt Collections is the sole producer and seller of Nile Valley Linens, which come in a variety of colors from the palest pastel to the darkest amethyst and burgundy.

Payment: PP, CC, MO, or CCk (PP preferred)
Positive Feedback Rating: 99.5%
Selling on eBay since 2003

The Silk Bedroom (eBay User ID: perfecteve)
Silk bedding

In 1999, a semester abroad took the owner of The Silk Bedroom to Asia and was the inspiration for her desire to bring Asia's silk products to eBay. The Silk Bedroom primarily provides quality silk bedding, including sheets, pillowcases, and duvet covers. These come in sizes from twin to king and California king, and in a variety of colors. An eBay Powerseller, The Silk Bedroom also offers some silk and lace lingerie and lovely Vietnamese kimonos as they become available.

Payment: PP, CC, MO, PCk, or CCk (PP preferred)
Positive Feedback Rating: 99.9%
Selling on eBay since 2000

Mich4280 (eBay User ID: mich4280)
Ralph Lauren bedding

Located in Georgia, Mich4280, an eBay Powerseller, specializes in individual items from the Ralph Lauren collection of fine linens. The offerings at auction are constantly changing, making Mich4280 the perfect eBay store to check when you want to round out a bedroom that is missing a sheet, pillow shams, or extra pillowcases—at discount prices.

Payment: PP, CC, MO, or CCk (PP preferred)
Positive Feedback Rating: 99.6%
Selling on eBay since 2003

Photo Courtesy of Indian Selections.

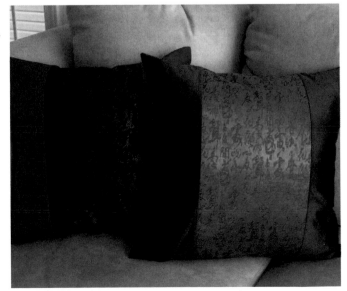

FabricGuru (eBay User ID: fabricguru)
Drapery and upholstery remnants

FabricGuru offers the Internet's largest selection of drapery and upholstery remnants. Upholstery remnants are available in chenille, damask, tapestry, leather, and more. The wide array of drapery remnants comes from design collections by Waverly, Covington, Laura Ashley, and many others. These remnants come in sizes ranging from one-yard to 16-yard pieces. FabricGuru, is committed to selling only first-quality remnants.

Payment: PP, or CC
Positive Feedback Rating: 99.6%
Selling on eBay since 2000

Crabdaddy's Deals (eBay User ID: crabdaddylonglegs)
Fabric remnants and trims

A part of FabricGuru's team, Crabdaddy's Deals offers upholstery and drapery fabric, toiles and silk fabrics, and high-end Italian fabrics. The store also carries outdoor fabrics; tropical, plaid, and animal prints; and an enormous array of decorative trims. With more than 25 years in the fabric business, FabricGuru and Crabdaddy's Deals are committed to offering quality fabric at great prices.

Payment: PP, or CC
Positive Feedback Rating: 99.3%
Selling on eBay since 1999

Touch of Europe (eBay User ID: touchofeurope)
Vintage linens

Touch of Europe, an eBay Powerseller, sells vintage European linens, small decorative pieces and some vintage clothing. The owner of the site spends weeks each year in Europe searching out unique, elegant, and romantic linens in France, Italy, Belgium, Holland, Germany, and the UK. These range from embroidered tablecloths to crocheted doilies to linen sheets, bedspreads, euro shams, even kitchen items. New items are added each week.

Payment: PP, CC, MO, CCk, or PCk
Positive Feedback Rating: 100%
Selling on eBay since 1999

Vintage Blessings (eBay User ID: vintageblessings)
Vintage quilts and linens

Inspired with a love of quilts by her grandmother, the owner of Vintage Blessings is committed to offering only the finest in antique quilts and linens. The store supplies a variety of vintage items. In addition to antique quilts, quilt tops, Amish quilts, embroidered napkins, lace table runners, crewel work, and schoolgirl samplers may be available at times. Quilts range in size from crib size to full bed size and come in a variety of patterns.

Payment: PP, CC, MO, PCk, or CCk (PP preferred)
Positive Feedback Rating: 100%
Selling on eBay since 1998

GB-Best Antique Quilts (eBay User ID: gb-best)
Antique quilts

GB-Best, an eBay Powerseller, supplies fine and unusual American handcrafts for the collector. The ever-changing items on the site include quilts, quilt tops, quilt blocks, Pennsylvania Dutch quilts, Pennsylvania crazy quilts, crib quilts, and appliquéd quilts. Shoppers may find samplers and other embroideries occasionally offered for sale, as they become available.

Payment: PP, CC, MO, PCk, or CCk
Positive Feedback Rating: 99.9%
Selling on eBay since 1998

Photo Courtesy of Indian Selections.

Precious Antiques Cargabı (eBay User ID: cargabı)

China, silver, crystal

Precious Antiques Cargab1, provides high-end silver, glass, porcelain, crystal, and other collectible items. The site provides very large photos of items for sale, which include Wedgwood, Lenox, Royal Copenhagen, Meissen, Limoges, Belleek, and others. In its large and changing collection, potential buyers might find German porcelain, Bohemian art glass, Sheffield William Adams silver, Reed and Barton spoons, Baccarat silver, even antique jewelry.

Payment: PP, CC, MO, PCk, or CCk (PP preferred)
Positive Feedback Rating: 99.3%
Selling on eBay since 2001

Fred Mandel (eBay User ID: fredmandel)

Antique pewter and silver

An eBay Powerseller, Fred Mandel handles fine antique pewter and silver collectibles. Bowls, candlesticks, pitchers, candle snuffers, tea sets, and plates abound on this site and are sold at unbeatable prices. Among them collectors may find rare items such as a child's porringer.

Payment: PP, CC, MO, PCk, or CCk
Positive Feedback Rating: 100%
Selling on eBay since 2004

My Tableware.com (eBay User ID: mytableware.com)
Replacement dinnerware

With over 23,000 listings, My Tableware.com is committed to providing pattern dinnerware, whether active or discontinued patterns, casual or formal place settings, available or vintage pieces. From their vast warehouse, they provide replacement pieces for brands such as Noritake, Royal Doulton, Wedgwood, Franciscan, Johnson Brothers, Spode, Lenox, Pfaltzgraff, Mikasa and many more. My Tableware.com, an eBay Powerseller, leaves no table setting incomplete.

Payment: PP, CC, MO, PCK, or CCk
Positive Feedback Rating: 99.8%
Selling on eBay since 1999

Replacements Ltd (eBay User ID: replacementsltd)
Replacement dinnerware and collectibles

In business over twenty years, Replacements Ltd carries more than ten million pieces in over 200,000 patterns in their enormous North Carolina showroom and warehouse. A supplier of both old and new china, they provide replacement pieces in active and also in discontinued fine porcelain dinnerware. Their site includes china, glass, silver, collector plates, and a vast array of high-end collectibles, providing such items as Wedgwood soup tureens, Fostoria glass, Gorham silver, Waterford stemware, Royal Doulton figurines, and Caithness glass paperweights among others.

Payment: CC (V, MC, D), MO, PCK, or CCk
Positive Feedback Rating: 99.7%
Selling on eBay since 1998

The Finders (eBay User ID: thefinders)
Lenox china

The Finders deals primarily in Lenox fine china, both new and retired patterns. Their site also features Lenox collectible figurines, Holiday Lenox, and ornaments. But The Finders is an eclectic and interesting store. Mixed in with their outstanding collection of Lenox, a buyer might find totebags, jackets, Chai mixes, closet hangers, even cookware and small appliances. The Finders is an eBay Powerseller.

Payment: PP, CC, MO, CCk
Positive Feedback Rating: 99.9%
Selling on eBay since 2001

Fine Glass Collection 88
(eBay User ID: fineglasscollection88)
Murano glass

Owned by an art collector who loves art glass and decided to sell as well as collect, Fine Glass Collection, an eBay Powerseller, offers a variety of Murano pieces with a focus on hand and mouth-blown vases and blown glass paperweights. Millefiori pieces are offered as well as art glass figures, all Murano, all beautiful, all Italian.

Payment: PP, CC, MO, PCk, or CCk
Positive Feedback Rating: 99.4%
Selling on eBay since 2004

Discount Oneida Flatware
(eBay User ID: discount-oneida-flatware)
Oneida flatware

As the name suggests, this site offers new and first quality Oneida flatware. It is the largest discount Oneida store on eBay and offers unbeatable prices and fast and efficient delivery. Discount Oneida Flatware, an eBay Powerseller, stocks all patterns from Act I to Wordsworth and all retired patterns from American Colonial to Whittier. In addition to complete sets and individual pieces of stainless, silver and silverplate flatware, they have a fine selection of serving pieces to complement any flatware set.

Payment: PP (preferred), CC, MO, CCk, or PCk
Positive Feedback Rating: 100%
Selling on eBay since 2000

Tomkat Collectibles (eBay User ID: Tomkat9er)
Depression glass

Tomkat is first and foremost a site for collectors of Depression glass with a large selection of pieces in blue, pink, green, amber, and lace crystal. The site also features elegant glassware and crystal by Fostoria, Caprice, and others. Jeanette Jadeite items for the kitchen are available. Tomkat, an eBay Powerseller, also discounts Pyrex, Fire King, and Corelle dinnerware, with a huge inventory of the latter.

Payment: CC, MO, PCk, CCk (PP preferred)
Positive Feedback Rating: 99.8%
Selling on eBay since 1999

Cady-Did (eBay User ID: cady-did)

Antique silver

Cady-Did offers antique silver flatware by Gorham, International, Lunt, Towle, Wallace, Stieff, and others. Sold as individual pieces, these antique spoons, butter spreaders, olive spoons, pickle forks, sauce ladles and meat forks (to name just a few possibilities) can round out a set or stand alone to enhance a table setting. Cady-Did, an eBay Powerseller, offers only flatware in excellent condition.

Payment: MO, PCk, or CCk
Positive Feedback Rating: 99.7%
Selling on eBay since 2000

Adila's Sterling (eBay User ID: adila1)

Silver

Adila's Sterling has been in business for twelve years and specializes in sterling silver flatware, holloware, tea and coffee sets, bowls, candlesticks and candelabras, platters, and more. An eBay Powerseller, her offerings are constantly changing and include rare and costly items for the discriminating collector.

Payment: MO, PCk, or CCk
Positive Feedback Rating: 99.7%
Selling on eBay since 2000

Silver Again (eBay User ID: silveragain)

Fine silver

Silver Again, an eBay Powerseller, specializes in sterling silver flatware, selling primarily antique vintage estate silver. While they may have some complete sets of silver, most items at auction are pieces, such as eight teaspoons or twelve forks. The site may also feature serving pieces, silver platters, antique hollowware, or occasionally a rare collectible—for example, a piece made of antique coin silver.

Payment: PP, CC, MO, PPc, or CCk
Positive Feedback Rating: 99.7%
Selling on eBay since 2002

Photo Courtesy of Jazzy Decor.

SFL Maven Fine Antiques, Etc. (eBay User ID: sflmaven)

Fine antiques

SFL Maven is a family-owned and operated online antique business located in southern Florida, where most of their collectibles are purchased. They carry a fine collection of outstanding pieces of Waterford glass, Sevres and Limoges China, Tiffany glass, Royal Doulton porcelain and Lladro figurines. Their site also is the place to find one-of-a-kind antique jewelry and all kinds of memorabilia.

Payment: PP, CC, MO, PPc, or CCk
Positive Feedback Rating: 100%
Selling on eBay since 2003

Douglasilver.com (eBay User ID: douglasilver)

New and estate silver

Douglasilver.com sells both estate and new silver flatware and serving pieces. Older pieces are polished by an expert silversmith or are unused jewelry stock. The site offers an extensive listing of exquisite silver flatware pieces by Towle, Wallace, Gorham, and many, many others. Vintage patterns and hard-to-find serving pieces are available, everything from olive spoons to asparagus servers. Some complete sets and some new sets may also be found at auction.

Payment: PP, or CC
Positive Feedback Rating: 99.6%
Selling on eBay since 1999

Art & Objects

Photo Courtesy of Classy Yet Affordable.

Accessories

etgs2000 (eBay User ID: etgs2000)
Classically designed room dividers
Some pieces offered by this seller include a room divider with a wrought-iron frame and a stain-resistant beige fabric, and another with an Asian-inspired bamboo print embedded in a natural pine finish frame. Many styles have a matching bench that is auctioned separately. etgs2000 also auctions tables, stools, chests, and sofa tables.

Payment: PP
Positive Feedback Rating: 100%
Selling on eBay since 2002

NOVICA.com (eBay User ID: novica.com)
Handmade pieces from artisans around the world
NOVICA, in association with National Geographic, is a global community of empowered artisans, and a leading source for handmade home décor. NOVICA auctions over 8,500 pieces from 1,700 artisans. It is one of the most comprehensive home décor sites on eBay—there are amazing product descriptions, great photos, in-depth artisan bios (including photos and links to other works by the artisan), customer reviews, and shipping information. To name just a fraction of what is for auction, NOVICA accessories include carved Peruvian wooden trunks, an African carved wall sculpture, antique leather world maps from Brazil, and a Thai teak carved elephant table. NOVICA also auctions original oil paintings from around the world.

Payment: PP, CC, MO, or CCk
Positive Feedback Rating: 99.7%
Selling on eBay since 1999

(eBay User ID: fmjr)
Antique stained glass windows

This eBay site auctions moderately priced stained glass windows. There is a strong attention to detail in these pieces—most have an ornate patterning and fine craftsmanship. The glass measures around 25" tall by 40" high and have start bids as low as $150.

Payment: PP, MO, PC, or CCk
Positive Feedback Rating: 99.7%
Selling on eBay since 1999

Photo Courtesy of Classy Yet Affordable.

Jazzy Décor (eBay User ID: jazzydecor)
Chinese-inspired table runners

Jazzy Décor creates sharp, Chinese-inspired home décor table runners. Their table runners are bold in color, in red, blue, fuchsia, and gold. Traditional Chinese designs include the double happiness, dragon patterns, and longevity lock patterns. Calligraphy sends messages like "blessed" and "long life." Matching tassels come with most runners.

Payment: PP, MO, or CCk
Positive Feedback Rating: 100%
Selling on eBay since 2002

Classy Yet Affordable (eBay User ID: classyyetaffordable)
Contemporary accessories

Classy Yet Affordable auctions accessories that you won't see elsewhere. Items for auction include a 3-piece iron and glass votive and mirror set, many types of metal wall art (including a sunflower and a metal forest), key hook storage cabinet, and fireplace screens. Classy Yet Affordable is a great site to visit when you have extra wall space that you'd like to decorate.

Payment: PP, CC, MO, or CCk
Positive Feedback Rating: 99.6%
Selling on eBay since 1998

Photo Courtesy of Big Moose Lodge.

The Palace Collection 2001
(eBay User ID: palaceproductions)
Wall sculpture, art prints, and decorative scrolls

The Palace Collection is owned and operated by artists who auction over 50 pieces through their eBay store, including sculptures and prints. Each piece is designed in one of three cultural traditions: Egyptian, Celtic, or Chinese. The Celtic designs are inspired by the Book of Kells—an ancient text, with illuminated artwork, that was created in Ireland circa 800. The Chinese designs combine ancient symbols and Chinese calligraphy, wishing homeowners peace, patience, and wisdom. The Egyptian designs are based on traditional Egyptian symbols, like the Eye of Hours (symbol of good luck and protection) and Ankh (symbol of eternal life). The wall sculptures are cast in stone and come with room in the back for easy wall mounting. All prints are reproduced by the artists on a fiber paper called Lokta paper, which is handmade in the Himalayas.

Payment: PP, MO, PC, or CCk
Positive Feedback Rating: 99.7%
Selling on eBay since 2001

Art Closeouts (eBay User ID: art-closeouts)
Framed reproduction prints

Art Closeouts frames art prints and auctions them with reasonable start bids. The prints arrive at your door, ready to hang. This framed artwork includes vintage ad prints from France, which look great on any wall. The product photos feature a close-up of the frame and a mock-up of the mounted print.

Payment: PP, CC, MO, PC, or CCk
Positive Feedback Rating: 99.4%
Selling on eBay since 2003

(eBay User ID: blueonc)
Reproduction prints

The lovely prints available through this site are auctioned in bundles of four to six prints. Simple scenes of a country farm, strawberries, or trout will add a whimsical touch to a bathroom or kitchen. Standard shipping means that on most auctions you won't spend more than $5 for prints that will enliven any space.

Payment: PP, MO, PC, or CCk
Positive Feedback Rating: 99.7%
Selling on eBay since 1999

Holland House Clocks (eBay User ID: hollandhouseclocks)
Grandfather clocks

All of the Chicago-based Holland House Clocks are handmade in Illinois. Each clock is constructed using hand-cut hardwoods. Holland House pays special attention to the finishing process—their clocks undergo as many as 18 finishing steps involving waxing and hand-rubbing the wood to a deep, rich patina. Weighing in at 200 lbs., the shipping for the clocks can be as high as $200, but it is well worth the cost for these well-constructed heirloom pieces.

Payment: PP, CC, MO, PC, or CCk
Positive Feedback Rating: 98.9%
Selling on eBay since 2001

Dawn's Bit of Everything (eBay User ID: dawns-bit-of-everything)
Fireplace accessories

Dawn's auctions great fireplace accessories, including screens, log holders, and bellows. Screens, available in satin chrome or polished brass, are functional and stylish. Log holders not only organize your space, they'll add to the charm of it. Bellows, those ingenious creations that allow you to manually pump air onto a fire, are hand-carved and come in pine or oak.

Payment: PP, CC, MO, PC, or CCk
Positive Feedback Rating: 100%
Selling on eBay since 2003

Nafe' Iron Works (eBay User ID: anne3261)
Iron finials, brackets, and paper towel holders

Nafe' Iron Works, based in Texas, designs iron wares for the home. Designs include an Italian iron paper-towel holder that won't turn over when you pull a towel off, cast iron architectural finials with a rust-like finish, and shelving brackets that double as plant hangers. Each of these pieces is designed with balance and wonderful form.

Payment: PP, CC, MO, PC, or CCk
Positive Feedback Rating: 99.9%
Selling on eBay since 2002

Big Moose Lodge (eBay User ID: bigmooselodge)
Mountain-inspired home décor

Big Moose Lodge auctions Adirondack-style home décor accessories. From log-wood framed mirrors, to pine-twig welcome signs, the accessories on this site are off the beaten path. Big Moose Lodge also carries rustic leather fringe throw pillows and Americana-themed accessories.

Payment: PP, CC, MO, PC, or CCk
Positive Feedback Rating: 100%
Selling on eBay since 2001

Jgmxxx (eBay User ID: jgmxxx)
Antique bronze

Jgmxxx is a specialist in bronze collectibles and art objects, offering everything from large bronze figures to ornate door knockers, barn door handles, wall sconces, and much, much more. Whether the buyer is looking for a bronze drawer pull or a statue of Mercury, this is the store to check.

Payment: PP, CC, MO, PCk, or CCk
Positive Feedback Rating: 99%
Selling on eBay since 2000

Anatolian Carpets and Artifacts
(eBay User ID: anatoliancarpetsandartifacts)
Imports from Turkey

A small business operating from Dalton, Georgia, Anatolian Carpets and Artifacts, an eBay Powerseller, imports all their items directly from Turkey. They specialize in handmade new, semi-antique, and antique Oriental carpets, and many beautiful ones are pictured, including some tribal rugs and a few Persian, Armenian, and Azerian examples. Their site, however, is not limited to carpets. They also import and sell ceramic tiles, hand-painted china, glass evil eyes with kilim strips, and antique copper items both large and small.

Payment: PP, CC, MO, PCk, or CCk
Positive Feedback Rating: 99.6%
Selling on eBay since 2000

Wooden Bowls by David Walsh
(eBay User ID: davidwalshbowlmaker)
Wooden bowls

David Walsh is an artist living and working in Pennsylvania. A full-time bowl turner, his work was formerly sold in galleries in 20 states. He uses only old trees of character, and all bowls are cut out of the log, rough-turned to their approximate shape, dried, and then finished. These fine pieces are copiously pictured on his site to show the bowl in detailed close-up both inside and out. David Walsh, who also makes some vases, is an eBay Powerseller.

Payment: PP, CC, MO, PCk, or CCk
Positive Feedback Rating: 99.6%
Selling on eBay since 2000

WWolst12 (eBay User ID: wwolst12)
High-quality collectibles

WWolst21, an eBay Powerseller, offers a variety of collectibles of high quality, from musical instruments to toys to jewelry. Serious and amateur collectors of antiques can often find something of interest on this eclectic site, whether it be a Folk Art figure, a 19th-century German violin, or a miniature drawing from Holland.

Payment: PP, MO, or PCk
Positive Feedback Rating: 99.8%
Selling on eBay since 1999

Congogrey (eBay User ID: congogrey)
Rare prints

Congogrey is the eBay version of Rare Prints Gallery.com. A collector of antique prints for over 20 years, Congogrey specializes in natural history, architecturals, cartography, and portraits, offering only prints of the highest quality. The collector may find pre-1900 prints by Audubon, George Edwards, Bivort, or Sweert, to name only a few. An eBay Powerseller, Congogrey boasts a perfect Feedback Rating.

Payment: PP, CC (V, MC), MO, or CCk (PP preferred)
Positive Feedback Rating: 100%
Selling on eBay since 1998

Fine Art Masters (eBay User ID: fineartmasters)
Modern and Contemporary fine art

Fine Art Masters provides high-quality modern and contemporary fine art prints, drawings, sculptures, and paintings at very low prices. They specialize in works by Miro, Picasso and Dali, but their offerings are not limited to those three artists. As they hold a No-Reserve auction on the first Wednesday of every month with bids starting at $9, a potential buyer needs to watch the site closely. Fine Art Masters is an eBay Powerseller.

Payment: PP, or CC (PP preferred)
Positive Feedback Rating: 99.7%
Selling on eBay since 2000

Russ Levin (eBay User ID: russlevin)
Photographs

Russ Levin was selling on eBay as RUSCAM, but is now selling under his own name. A photographer, himself, he has been a collector of fine photography since the 1970s and operates a gallery in Monterey, California. He offers a variety of carefully chosen photographs by himself, Brett Weston, John Sexton, John Wimberley and others. He hopes to add works by Tom Milea, Henry Gilpin, Martha Casenove, Ryuijie, and others in the near future.

Payment: CC (V, MC) MO, PPk, or CCk
Positive Feedback Rating: 99.9%
Selling on eBay since 1998

Antique Majolicas (eBay User ID:antiquemajolicas)
Majolica tiles

Antique Majolicas, as the name indicates, sells antique Art Nouveau majolica tiles. With a huge inventory of over 600 tiles in many styles, designs, and colors, there is something to please every collector. All tiles are pictured in great detail and give the tile's provenance to the degree that it is known.

Payment: PP, CC, MO, PCk, or CCk
Positive Feedback Rating: 99.6%
Selling on eBay since 2002

Cashco1000 (eBay User Id: cashco1000)
Themed home décor

Cashco1000 began as a hobby but has developed into a thriving eBay business. An eBay Powerseller, Cashco1000 specializes in themed decorating items—cowboys, flamingos, frogs, apples, tropical fish, grapes, angels, and many, many more. The buyer searching for a themed comforter set, toilet seat, clock, teapot, salt and pepper shaker set, wallpaper, or lighting fixture stands a good chance of finding it on Cashco1000.

Payment: PP, CC, MO, PCk, or CCk (PP preferred)
Positive Feedback Rating: 99.9%
Selling on eBay since 1999

Liberty Clock Company (eBay User Id: brian.ray)
Handmade clocks

Based in Arizona, Liberty Clock Company makes and sells handmade wall clocks. Most are antique reproductions. The clocks come in a variety of sizes, many as large as 36" in diameter. The buyer can choose the color and whether or not to add a pendulum or a working second hand. In addition, the clock can be personalized.

Payment: PP, MO, or CCk
Positive Feedback Rating: 99.8%
Selling on eBay since 2000

Lords and Company (eBay User ID: lordscollections)
Silk flower sand trees

Lords and Company has been in the wholesale silk flower business since 1981, and brought their silk flowers to eBay in 1999. They offer very realistic, unusual and high-end silk trees and flowers, as well as original designer arrangements. Trees, such as fountain palm and mango, are pre-potted, pre-mossed and pre-shaped while stems and arrangements come with a vase. Based in California, Lords and Company is an eBay Powerseller.

Payment: PP, CC, MO, PCk, or CCk
Positive Feedback Rating: 99.8%
Selling on eBay since 1999

Frames

Western Traditions (eBay User ID: texartnow)
Rusticated photo frames

Western traditions auctions handcrafted wood and metal photography frames. Wooden frames come in dozens of forms, including flat and crown molding styles. There are multiple sizes to choose from and the company offers to take custom orders. Frames are very inexpensive, but you'll need to purchase the glass and frame hardware separately, which you can do directly through Western Traditions' eBay store.

Payment: PP, CC, MO, PC, or CCk
Positive Feedback Rating: 99.8%
Selling on eBay since 2003

Picture Frames Store (eBay User ID: debandya)
Contemporary photo frames

The Picture Frames Store auctions great frames from well-known manufacturers like Burnes of Boston. For tabletops or walls, the frames are made of wood or metal, and come in eight different sizes. Bring the family portrait to work or frame the panoramic of your favorite vista. Or bid on their diploma-sized frames and finally mount your important certifications.

Payment: PP, MO, or CCk
Positive Feedback Rating: 99.7%
Selling on eBay since 2003

Framed 4 Good (eBay User ID: woode59)
Solid mahogany photo frames

The frames on this site are simple yet elegant. They are hand-crafted from solid mahogany and are finished with three coats of polyurethane. Each frame comes complete with glass, plywood backing, and a notch for wall mounting. Make your own matte backing or let the photo rest in the wooden frame on its own. Sizes include 4" x 6" and 8" x 10".

Payment: PP, MO, or CCk
Positive Feedback Rating: 100%
Selling on eBay since 2002

Paris Variety (eBay User ID: elvibora)
Contemporary glass photo frames

Paris Variety auctions striking beveled and etched glass photo frames. These frames add a simple elegance while keeping your photographs safe. They come in an array of styles, including vertically curved, horizontally-curved, or the traditional flat frame. Sizes range from 5" x 7" to 8" x 10", and 7" x 5" to 10" x 8".

Payment: PP, CC, MO, PC, or CCk
Positive Feedback Rating: 100%
Selling on eBay since 1999

Annie's Workshop (eBay User ID: anniesworkshop)
Stately frames

Annie's Workshop auctions photo frames from Tizo Design, Inc. These frames are designed carefully, from the detailing on the face of the frame to the beautiful backs. These are perfect frames for sofa tables, where both sides of the frame are visible because the backs of the frames are enameled in bronze. All frames have a shapely stand and fleur-de-lis braces. The slightly higher start bids for these frames are well worth it—they're beautiful, they will keep your most valuable photographs safe, and are sure to last a long time.

Payment: PP, MO, PC, or CCk
Positive Feedback Rating: 99.9%
Selling on eBay since 1998

The Decorator's Touch (eBay User ID: teritowe)
Antique reproduction photo frames

The ornate frames on this site will add a touch of Old World charm to your home. Many, like the "Fleur de Lis," are designed with ornate scroll-work and are painted to resemble the patina of aged bronze. There are also less ornate wooden frames whose delicately hand-painted edges are meant to evoke a Parisian bistro. The Decorator's Touch also carries an assortment of accessories for the home, like throw pillows and candle holders.

Payment: PP, CC, MO, PC, or CCk
Positive Feedback Rating: 99.9%
Selling on eBay since 2000

Vases

Photo Courtesy of Classy Yet Affordable.

Minerva Crystal Fossil Stone Shop (eBay User ID: pjbiskup)

Striated onyx vases

The vases on this site are turned from one solid piece of banded onyx. They are approximately 2 1/4" tall, have a 2" diameter, and are available in either round or oval shapes. Each piece consists of different colored bands that wrap around the diameter, including sienna, beige, cream, yellow, grey, and orange. The bands are not only beautiful, they're also geological records of a place and time in the earth's history. No two pieces are exactly alike.

Payment: PP, CC, MO, PC, or CCk
Positive Feedback Rating: 99.9%
Selling on eBay since 1999

Unique Acquisitions (eBay User ID: uniqueacquisitions)

Shapely porcelain vases

There are dozens of porcelain vases for auction through Unique Acquisitions. These elegant pieces are inspired by the early 20th-century Art Nouveau movement. They are handcrafted from fine clays and glazes, and have nature-inspired raised relief images. At almost 12", these pieces are impressively sized and will provide a bold decorating statement.

Payment: PP, MO, or CCk
Positive Feedback Rating: 99.7%
Selling on eBay since 2001

More Than Nature (eBay User ID: onyxguys)

Golden onyx vases

From Java Island, these onyx vases are golden in color. They have a clean look, with few veins and just a few muted colors. Their well-polished exteriors make them appear to glow. Whether filled with flowers or left empty, these pieces will bring elegance and natural refinement to any space.

Payment: PP, CC, MO, PC, or CCk
Positive Feedback Rating: 100%
Selling on eBay since 2003

Abc78333 (eBay User ID: Abc78333)

Murano glass vases

Glorious Murano glass vases and paperweights; glass sculptures of cats and peacocks, penguins, and clownfish; and lovely gemstone globes make this eBay store a browser's delight. Regular auctions are held and abc78333 is an eBay Powerseller.

Payment: PP, CC, MO, CCk, or PCk (PP preferred)
Positive Feedback Rating: 99.2%
Selling on eBay since 1999

Rebeccas_Unique_Glass
(eBay User ID: rebeccas_unique_glass)

Glass collectibles

Rebeccas_Unique_Glass, an eBay Powerseller, offers unusual art glass. Some, but not all, is Italian Murano glass. The site features vases, glass figurines, paperweights, bowls, and a wide assortment of glass flowers. Some pieces are antiques, others primarily great finds.

Payment: PP, CC, MO, PCk, or CCk (PP preferred)
Positive Feedback Rating: 99.6%
Selling on eBay since 2001

INDEX